V-RAY MY WAY

V-RAY MY WAY

A Practical Designer's Guide to Creating Realistic Imagery Using V-Ray & 3ds Max

LEE WYLDE

Focal Press
Taylor & Francis Group

NEW YORK AND LONDON

First published 2014
by Focal Press
70 Blanchard Road, Suite 402, Burlington, MA 01803

and by Focal Press
2 Park Square, Milton Park, Abingdon, Oxon OX14 4RN

Focal Press is an imprint of the Taylor & Francis Group, an informa business

Library of Congress Cataloging in Publication Data
Wylde, Lee.
   V-Ray my way : a practical designer's guide to creating realistic imagery using
   V-Ray & 3ds Max / Lee Wylde.
      pages cm
   1. V-R ay. 2. 3ds max (Computer file) 3. Architectural rendering—
   Computer-aided design. I. Title.
   NA2728.W98 2014
   776'.7—dc23   2013038376

ISBN: 978-0-415-70963-7 (pbk)
ISBN: 978-1-315-88544-5 (ebk)

Typeset in AGaramond and Avenir
By Keystroke, Station Road, Codsall, Wolverhampton

Printed and bound in India by Replika Press Pvt. Ltd.

For Jovan, and what could have been …

Bound to Create

You are a creator.

Whatever your form of expression — photography, filmmaking, animation, games, audio, media communication, web design, or theatre — you simply want to create without limitation. Bound by nothing except your own creativity and determination.

Focal Press can help.

For over 75 years Focal has published books that support your creative goals. Our founder, Andor Kraszna-Krausz, established Focal in 1938 so you could have access to leading-edge expert knowledge, techniques, and tools that allow you to create without constraint. We strive to create exceptional, engaging, and practical content that helps you master your passion.

Focal Press and you.

Bound to create.

We'd love to hear how we've helped you create. Share your experience:
www.focalpress.com/boundtocreate

Focal Press
Taylor & Francis Group

CONTENTS

ACKNOWLEDGMENTS

Thank you to the following individuals for their careful review of the text during its various stages of development:

Clark Cory, Alex Huguet Paredes, Jeremy Sahlman, and Matthew Valero.

Thanks also to Christian Bloch from HDRlabs.com for allowing me to use some of their HDR lighting files for the exercises. Thank you to Markus Huber from openfootage.net for generously allowing me to use his HDRI files within some of the scenes.

And finally to my wife for her support and for keeping my energetic children entertained for the duration of my writing.

CHAPTER 1

MY EXPERIENCE AND BACKGROUND STORY

'To infinity and beyond', the instantly recognizable phrase that shaped the public's perception of computer visualization forever.

It was at the time of the release of the first *Toy Story* movie that I was sat in rural England in a small town called Sheffield, wondering what I wanted to do with my life. At 15 years old who actually knows what they want to do in life? However, Woody, Buzz and the rest of the gang had me mesmorized and keen to discover more about this phenomenal art.

At 15 I was the youngest in my year at high school. I had always been creative and teachers would often hurl abuse at me for doodling during history or religious education classes.

I had a computer at home and was taking computer classes at school, but these were nothing compared to the industry that was out there in the real world.

Luckily one day I was in a high street retail store and came across a magazine called *3D World*. It was packed to the brim with industry information and glossy renderings of characters, creatures and vehicles, and I knew that this was my starting point.

The publication contained tutorials, albeit a little advanced for me but nevertheless incredibly useful. The most useful aspect was the CD-ROM with 30 day trial software that I yearned for every month. This was perfect, an ideal way to learn the very basics at my own pace. I spent the next six months glued to my rather slow, rather inefficient Acer laptop following the steps to create meshes, render flowers and model spaceships.

My dedication and inquisitiveness had led me part of the way into a new career; however I was not prepared for the next stage of my life.

In the year 2000 I was accepted onto the British Government's Modern Apprenticeship Scheme. I joined a bustling architectural practice called Hadfield Cawkwell Davison. This was a new world to me; there were roughly 70 people in the company. Each studio was filled with architectural models, building materials, fabric samples, drawings and lots of coffee. My position was as an architectural apprentice.

With my pen in my shirt pocket I arrived on my first day ready to design the next building worthy of the architect of the year award. My ambition was strong but the likelihood of winning architect of the year was fairly low.

I soon came across the graphics department, a group of long-haired designers who listened to 1980s' music with Starbucks cups on their desks. I was in awe and wanted to move in as soon as possible. At this time the production of artwork for architectural projects consisted of hand-drawn scanned images, digitally finished in Photoshop. Nostalgically mounted on the walls were the most beautiful hand-drawn and water-colored architectural illustrations.

I was desperate to join this department but it was not to be, well not for a year and a half anyhow.

For those agonizing 18 months I was responsible for archiving, photocopying and tea-making. How fruitful life seemed. On the other hand the social aspect was amazing, I moved to different departments to help the interior designers. During the 18 months I managed to teach myself 3D Studio Max and AutoCAD.

The department had a copy of 3D Studio Max which at this time was version 3. I was granted access to the dongle during the studio's downtime (which was after 5:30 p.m.).

The practice did send me on training days for AutoCAD, but this was only 2D, and as ambitious as I was back then, I wanted 3D training.

I was in a position where I had to prove myself, yet not look as though I was above my station. One of the partners at the practice was very hands on, constantly mixing with the design team and providing creative direction. I knew this was the person I had to impress.

I had secretly modeled a whole building in 3D of a current project and had managed to render the facade and add trees and pavements etc. Looking back now they were dismal, but just what I needed to progress in my career. The practice, like others all over the UK at that time used an external consultant for high-end visualizations.

Having presented my boss with the output he was genuinely surprised that I had created the images. I showed him the files and explained how I had achieved the end result. I soon started to work on interior schemes and moved to the interior design department. From that day I was sent on my way to learn parts of professionally accredited 3D courses for intermediate and advanced 3D Studio Max users. Happy days.

During 2002 the incredibly annoying user-friendly 3D program was released called SketchUp. Architects at the time were praising the software and thought it was the best thing since sliced bread. I hated it. (I do not now, I find it a key part of my workflow). Having learned the technical aspects of 3D Studio Max I felt threatened that suddenly everyone could produce 3D with relative ease. Versatile, unique, with customizable outputs, no render times, SketchUp was industry-changing.

Once the management had figured out the time to create visuals using 3D Studio Max versus the time taken using SketchUp, well let's say I was less than pleased when I was told to use SketchUp instead.

Reluctantly I found myself using SketchUp almost every day for the remainder of my four years with the practice. I developed my own way of working, from taking briefs to photographing textures, making briefing sheets and eventually by default, setting up the company 3D department. It was fun, and that was the most important thing. I did not want to be an architect or an interior designer at that time, I had forgotten about climbing the career ladder. I simply enjoyed my creative time working with others to deliver stunning graphics for client meetings.

Come 5:30 p.m. we would be hooking everyone's machines up to try and figure out how to network render using 3D Studio Max. It certainly gave the IT department something new to experiment with. We were using 3D Studio Max more and more as production software after SketchUp had been pushed as far as it possibly could.

Back then we thought that the light tracer function was a gigantic breakthrough for us to use. When I look back now it makes me laugh, there were studios in the US and London using all sorts of wizardry and we had not a clue, we were in a bubble, but at least it was fun for us to explore and develop our skills.

We spent hours, days and weekends reading through online tutorials, reading through training manuals purchased from high street book stores and just generally experimenting. Books were virtually useless to us. They were too scientific, academic if you will. We needed fresh, industry-related direction.

That is the first lesson in life that I had learned, nothing is easy, or otherwise everyone would be doing it. I had developed my skills in texturing, lighting and modeling

enough to be able to create large scenes for leading retailers in the UK.

Finding Nemo was released in the UK during this year which quantified my admiration for Pixar, and how I longed to be the tea boy at their studios if given the chance. In fact I think I would be their tea boy now if I could wander in and out of each department looking at their stunning artwork.

'3D is a fad, there is no future in it, you are wasting your time.' The parting words from a member of staff as I left my first job to join another leading design practice in the UK.

I decided to depart from my first job for a number of reasons. I thoroughly enjoyed my creative days there; however I was young and had not grasped the corporate side of the working environment. With suits on one side of the office and Hawaiian shirts on the other, it was not exactly a recipe for a balanced workplace. At 19 years old I wanted to broaden my horizons and decided the best thing to do was to take my capabilities elsewhere.

In 2005 I started my own company called Foothill Studios. I was 20 and full of energy ready to make my company work. I had seen the invoices from 3D consultants in my first job and thought to myself that I could provide a similar service much cheaper.

I had no idea what I was getting myself into, but it felt great at the time, a real sense of adventure. With my glossy business cards ready, functioning website ready and price list ready it was time to market myself.

The great thing about the UK is that you can cold call and with a little tenacity can actually speak to the people you need to in order to pitch yourself. The decision makers if you will. This worked remarkably well for me and literally within the first week I had three projects to deliver.

My main aim at that time was to target architects, private property developers and interior designers throughout the UK. I created endless spreadsheets of business hit lists and allocated myself a time per week to speak to each one.

At the time I was mainly funded by the Bank of Mum and Dad; my father and I had built a new loft-space on my parents' house and I used it to operate my small studio from.

I had a unique style that I could pitch to clients; this combined with value for money certainly made me relevant to small and medium enterprises (SMEs). For the first year my clients mainly consisted of interior designers, architects and developers. This was a fantastic market at the time; developments were springing up all over the UK and all required artwork for planning authority approvals, marketing, public information etc.

One of the pivotal moments at this time came when I was contacted by a reputable furniture designer and manufacturer based in London. They had seen my work through a third party who had specified their furniture in a concept pitch.

After making inquiries the company had managed to track me down, where at the time I was fast asleep in bed after a whole night of rendering. Watching scan-lines come down my screen, just waiting for errors I had made, forcing me to re-render was tiresome work back then.

It was my mother who had come running up three flights of stairs yielding the wireless phone in her hand. 'There is a lovely man on the phone from London, he wants to talk to you about your work.'

I was half asleep and wearing *The Matrix* pajamas at the time. I do not think my professionalism was in question from what I was wearing, rather perhaps from my mother's interrogation of my potential client.

I was asked to travel to London the following week to meet the company in their very posh and rather swanky showroom in Clerkenwell. I lived three hours north of London and had only been there on vacation a few times. There was something about the place that electrified my aspirations.

My meeting was with the global account manager and a few other members of the design team. I had not realized at this point in my life just how significant the commercial furniture industry was.

My mother must have made a good impression as the first question was 'How is your Mother?'. I spent hours discussing their current range of office furniture, their visualization requirements and how knowledgeable I was with their catalogues.

Luckily I was very knowledgeable, for I had modeled their furniture from 2D drawings for other clients to produce 3D mock-up images. It was far more cost effective for me to provide clients with renderings of furniture systems rather than have the system transported, erected, photographed, dismantled and delivered back to their showroom.

The meeting was incredibly successful. Armed with numerous brochures, samples and their supplier contacts directory I returned to the train for a three-hour journey north.

Within a few days, much to the dismay of my father, furniture items started arriving at my parents' house, for my reference.

It seemed I was going to need a bigger boat. Along with the furniture were requisitions for 3D furniture mock-ups for projects throughout the country. I had more work than I had estimated for in my business plan. In fact I had exceeded my targets by more than 300 percent.

The contact list of suppliers, distributors and other companies was a fantastic opportunity for me to grow. The list comprised of over 50 companies throughout the UK all potentially requiring my services.

It took three months to contact all companies and to pitch to them. I had immediate success and found myself creating new material for retail projects, commercial projects and high-end branded interiors. This is where I learned my second big lesson in life.

I had more work than I could cope with. My machine at the time had been kindly donated by my first employer. I had upgraded the RAM but that was all I could do for it. Inevitably it needed replacing to handle the amount of rendering work I had to carry out. I was also receiving requests for animations.

I needed new kit. Lesson number two; do not rush into anything, research thoroughly.

Given the need for speed at this time and not wanting to have delays with other clients I ordered shiny new machines from BOXXTECH in the US. The kit cost an arm and a leg. It arrived on Christmas Eve, how fitting. My father had signed for the boxes and was less than pleased that stacks of boxes were taking up his living space. 'What the bloody hell is all this?'.

He thought that one computer should last forever and that my old machine should still be able to do the job. 'New machines, Dad, make more money.' Enough said, he was fine with the justification.

Onwards and upwards, I had unpacked all the elements. Brushed aluminum render servers lay glittering on my bedroom floor. The modeling machine was an impressive 16 GB RAM dual quad core beast. I kept my old machine in the corner for post-production work.

Now I had the necessary tools, I needed to really progress and deliver higher quality work. I wanted to pitch for animation projects, architectural, vehicle and product design etc. I had little experience in animation, but being young and tenacious I proceeded to punch above my weight.

'Lee, someone is on the phone from America!', the words my father was shouting from three floors down. Unlike my mother who would have dashed up three flights of stairs, my father took a more practical approach to announcing client calls.

It seems my decision to pitch above my comfort level had paid off; my first international client from the US. They required a 15-minute animation of a cruise liner with dolphins jumping out of the water, retracting marina, jet skis and all sorts of crazy elements. I didn't have a clue how on earth I was going to do it, so naturally I said yes.

I do not have many regrets in life, but looking back this had a firm place on the regret pile. This project should have been undertaken by a London-based studio with 10 latte-drinking animators packing state-of-the-art machinery and a monster render farm at their disposal.

Nope, it was to be undertaken by myself. With my dog at my side, who was often my strongest critic I must say, I began to come up with strategies to complete the project. I was incredibly good at planning and setting key stage deliverables and timelines for design projects.

With an overwhelming sense of commitment to the client, I made two lists. One list had elements of the projects I could do without using Uncle Google to fill me in on the bits I lacked the knowledge to complete. The other list, which at this point was demoralizingly larger than the other and often referred to as the how on earth list, contained things like ocean water, high dynamic range imaging (HDRI) lighting, pool water, moving people and most importantly how I was going to render the final image sequence.

During 2006 I went on a date (not just one I might add) and we found ourselves at the movies. *Poseidon* was the movie, which was about an ocean liner that was caught up in a catastrophic event, overturned and unfortunately for its inhabitants it sank, the usual boating accident film, but the visual effects were amazing.

There is a sequence at the beginning of the film where the camera pans around the periphery of the ship and zooms into the deck and finishes in a luxury cabin.

This was it; my inspiration had been burned into my memory. I think I must have viewed the trailer more than 100 times. With the vision in mind I set about creating the environment containing the water and main light source, so I could prepare the main vessel in another 3D Studio Max file, texture it and simply merge it into the lighting rig.

I often worked like this; it made sure that I had control over the lighting individually without affecting the main model. The main headache in the project so far was the ocean.

Plug-ins were available such as Real-Flow, which was way out of my price range, coupled with the fact that I would have to learn the software from scratch in time to deliver the project.

I trawled the web for resources, and spent hours and hours posting questions on forums. One day I came across a simulation software called Reactor. After using Uncle Google to find where I could buy the software, I found out I already had it, built into 3D Studio Max, doughnut.

After a week I was able to take the ship's hull and animate it cutting through an ocean plane to create what is known as wake. I also had to animate the ocean plane with noise and current. It was a fantastic learning process. I finally had the ocean liner textured, the manufacturers forwarded me a huge 200 MB zipped file containing the ship's 3D engineering model, it required significant cleaning and partial remodeling. I do like to make work hard for myself and chose to animate the ship during the early evening so I could insert artificial lights into the cabins and ship's hull for maximum contrast.

I must have thought I was in Hollywood. The test renders were actually rather good, the client was extremely happy. At 1920 × 1080 HD in 3D Studio Max's output preset, the render time was 15 minutes a frame.

It suddenly dawned on me just how long this project would take to render, at 24 frames per second and each frame taking 15 minutes, which was something like 21,600 frames to render in total. I had calculated that it would take 5400 hours or rather 225 days to render.

Doomed I was, but still resourceful I toyed with the idea of using an external consultant to render my scenes. I did find a render farm in the UK who could render my animation over a 395-hour period. The only issue was that it would cost me $13,000.

This was one of the most important lessons of my career, managing client expectations and managing your own expectations. Being young and resilient I managed to scrape a deal with the client.

I forwarded all of the final files with test renders that were pre-approved for production. I also included a list of suitable render farms that I had contacted beforehand and briefed about the design account. Luckily I had a very understanding client, not many are like this, especially in the current market. It was probably one of the most important lessons learned, if you want to do Hollywood effects, go to Hollywood, otherwise keep it grounded and achievable.

The closest I ever got to Hollywood was Kansas City. In 2007 I was contacted by Winntech through Coroflot. com, which is a free online portfolio website. I highly recommend it.

The position the company offered me was as an industrial designer of which I knew nothing about. Yet again being young and resilient, and knowing it had something to do with 3D, I went for it.

During the first couple of weeks at Winntech, I started to notice what makes America America. Coming from a background where design is so segregated and follows a hierarchy, I soon learned that I would have to adapt to the more socially inclusive design process, as practiced by the Americans.

Having come from a self-employed background and more familiar with spectrum of operational aspects of a design business, I admit that I found it difficult to just focus on one element of design in my position.

All designers are judged by the work that they produce, and having operated my own studio for so long, I was used to taking the credit for my work directly from clients. Suddenly I was in an environment where all of my and my coworkers' ideas were on the table, so you could say I felt protective about my concepts. I soon learned that designers to tend to gain bruised egos from being open to such scrutiny in all aspects of their work.

Over a three-month period, I understood just how strong and efficient their approach to design was, compared to the one I was used to. In other areas of the world, companies hire two or three designers to cope with a whole range of supporting design services. What I particularly liked about working in the US was the availability of a design team member for each part of the design process.

On a typical design account for a blue chip company, there would be one design account manager, one graphic designer, one interior designer and relative supporting staff. In order for the work we were producing to remain relevant, the account manager could pick and choose the designers that worked best together, which was ultimately highly beneficial to the client, thus reducing the amount of friction between the team. Producing visuals under this design regime was simple, because I knew exactly what was required and furthermore I could track and request information as I needed it. This was the same for the rest of the team; they would simply go away and do what was needed.

Out of all the design companies and agencies that I have worked for, Winntech has to be my favorite in terms of team effort and collaboration style. It's an ethos I try to utilize throughout my career even to this day.

Unfortunately my time in the US was cut short due to the government's visa system and as such I had to relocate and find work elsewhere.

In 2008 I landed in Dubai, which was an architect's paradise at that time. I was flown out to Dubai by one of Canada's largest, if not the largest, branding agency called Watt International, for the position of Mid Weight Retail Interior Designer.

I expected a grand arrival and an office fit for a CEO; however as this was a new satellite office I was sat in what can only be described as a luxurious prison cell with 15 other people. It turns out that most of the competitors were working like this, also due to the astronomical operating expenses.

Not only had I just gotten use to the streamlined work process in the US, I had to now forget that and work to a more custom Middle Eastern way of working.

When you think of 3D visuals, you think of one house, perhaps a villa, maybe even a hotel interior that you would simply complete, print out and hand over to your client. You cannot comprehend how important 3D visuals are until you have visited Dubai.

Dubai's whole property industry has been fuelled by 3D visuals. I often hear the statement that people don't read plans in Dubai. In my experience, this could not be further from the truth.

In such a bustling market, property developers rely heavily on visualizations in order to market their properties off-plan (before the structures are built). Many people, including consumers, do not read architectural plans with such a keen eye as a designer, so if this trend is happening in the UAE, then it certainly will be happening in other regions of the world. A picture, however, can sell a product or property within seconds, with no scope for error from the readers side.

This is why computer generated imagery is incredibly important within such markets and reflects why your attention to details truly makes a difference.

In order to see true investable value, those developers were investing millions of dollars in the production of 3D visuals, animations and walk-throughs in order to secure sales deals and raise general awareness of key developments in the city.

Clearly, it worked. Without a doubt, there is not a billboard in the UAE that doesn't have a 3D visual displayed on it. So the next time you are wondering what will be your future career pathway in 3D, just believe there is more to do out there other than visualizing your neighbor's house.

Since I have been residing in the UAE, I have worked for and consulted with some of the largest architectural and interior design companies in the Middle East. It's one of the most challenging places I have worked in terms of taking a brief, developing a concept and physically building a project. To work in this country you need to forget everything you know, adapt and realign your skills to suit. Why am I still here? I truly believe that in this current climate, considering the financial crisis the world is facing, the UAE is the only place that can offer stability, potential and career fulfillment as well as a jolly good salary.

Currently, I am the Head of Design at a Dubai based interior design agency and I am working on a multitude of commercial, retail, leisure and hospitality projects. I now face the challenge of developing my junior staff into process-driven and not product-orientated design individuals.

Hopefully this book will help you in developing your career further by showing you the quickest, practical way to visualize, which will enable you to travel the world and fulfill your potential.

CHAPTER 2

METHODOLOGY (HOW TO USE THIS BOOK)

In the design industry it is essential to possess the suitable equipment in order to complete the task in hand. When I sat down to write this book I believed that the book's exercises should be able to be accessed, reconfigured and rendered using everyday technology. I wanted to take a laptop from a generic high street retailer and use it to create the scenes and renders to prove that you do not need to spend thousands of dollars to create high-end visuals.

In the end I settled for a Dell and I must say I certainly have put the poor notebook through its paces and it has evidently performed. Here are the specifications:

Dell N5510
8 GB RAM,
64-BIT OPERATING SYSTEM.
WINDOWS 7
INTEL (®) CORE i7-2670QM CPU @ 2.20GHz

Now provided you set up your scenes to handle the amount of power available to you at hand, then you should be able to deliver realistic renders on time in line with this book's exercises. On the other hand if you are using a machine with a single processor and 2 GB of RAM, then I wouldn't promise your design manager visuals within two hours if I were you.

I have written this book to accommodate and cater for a wide range of design industry professionals and other user groups. Each exercise has been split into relevant sections highlighting preparation work, modeling, lighting, rendering and where necessary post-production work. It has been written in a way that supports my workflow, so if you fall asleep after working 18 hours on your project, you can wake up as fresh as a daisy and continue with the next section without forgetting where you were!

My particular way and method of working ensures that I cover all aspects of the design process so that the overall design intent does not suffer from last minute workloads, or mad rushes to simply get something out of the studio.

If you have a design account to visualize an architect's masterpiece, then you have to take into consideration that this piece of work represents a person's career, so you are going to want to do a thorough job.

Capturing and building a detailed scale model can take too long in 3D Studio Max alone. I highly suggest using SketchUp.

Within SketchUp there are numerous easy to use toolsets enabling you to work rapidly and to constantly be thinking of detail. Not only does SketchUp have its own workflow simplicities but it is also a great platform to show your clients progress. For the interior designers out there, my experience with SketchUp has proven to be incredibly successful.

The software enables designers to engage with clients on a new level allowing real-time walkthroughs and progressive changes to be made with relative ease.

More importantly clients feel that they are part of a process and that you are good value for money. I use this method all the time; it works and once the SketchUp is signed off you can then drop it straight into 3D Studio Max.

SketchUp seamlessly integrates into 3D Studio Max, making Max the perfect production tool for lighting and rendering.

You may already have your own workflow, which is fine; you can simply follow the exercises in this book to achieve your desired result.

CHAPTER 3

INTRODUCTION TO MY WORKFLOW

When it comes to creating photo-realistic renders you need to have a workflow. I know this can sound over the top; however without a plan and a method of achieving the desired end result; you will no doubt drive yourself crazy by not being focused.

If you have read my background story you will see that having a workflow where you use specific software for parts of the design process can save you time and significant expense.

My way of working ensures that I cover all aspects of the design intent and that it is effectively executed. My process is fairly simple. I use it wherever I can, whether it is for creating visuals or if I am designing a structure or interior space. The four-stage process goes something like this: (3.1)

Define > Design > Refine > Deliver

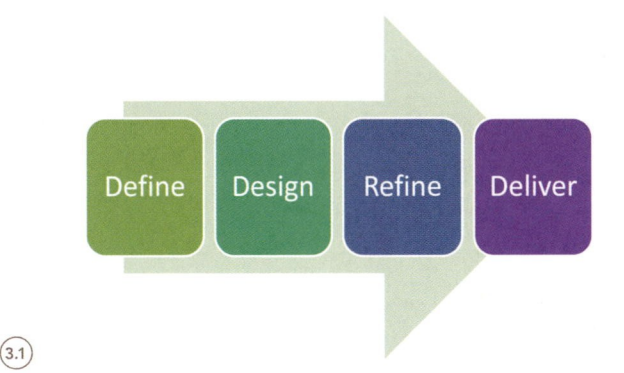

(3.1)

These four words become the backbone to all of my projects. Let's take a look at what each one actually means.

Defining a design problem is essential. What have you been hired for? It is not just about defining the problem but also about defining the parameters that will dictate your creative response. This usually includes an initial client briefing and building any conceptual development notes that have been mutually agreed upon.

The Define stage is also a suitable platform to establish fees, discuss required project timelines, discuss and explore essential design development information such as as-built drawing information or architects' drawings, brand packs etc. and to undertake a fairly comprehensive question and answer session.

Usually I create a briefing document ensuring that all the collated information from the client engagement session has been noted, explained and referenced in order for other members of the team to access and understand.

The Design stage is the main time-consuming period of the design process: sifting through AutoCAD files, making sure that they are all to scale and then purging and auditing to make sure they can be used in other software applications.

During this stage the base building model will be built including all necessary details to ensure a solid detailed rig is ready for the next stage.

I use SketchUp at this point to export very clean images highlighting key areas that need progressive approval. Engaging the client like this helps to build a solid relationship and also shows just how much work goes into visualization. In a way you educate them also.

Once everything has been modeled and signed off I then progress to the next step of creating custom shaders.

With the detailed model imported into 3D Studio Max I set about creating primary and secondary materials. Primary materials are the easiest to make, stone, concrete etc. Secondary materials take much longer to effectively create and UVW map. Materials such as alternate timbers, aluminum, steel, custom maps for branding and grass etc.

Depending on the size and type of scene I will usually have my own materials libraries to hand. In the interest of diversity I will create one-off materials for different clients.

I usually have a clear idea at the Define stage as to what I want the lighting to be like. This also helps me in the modeling stages. If I am producing a daytime scene then I need to make sure the lighting and shaders will perform and correctly portray the architecture in a positive way.

If I am producing evening scenes then I need to make sure that I have the correct peripheral lighting elements modeled and that they are properly referenced with IES lighting files etc.

Camera work I usually leave until the last stage so that I can see not only how the forms and surfaces interact but also to aid in the correct placement of peripheral items for general composition purposes.

Initial renders will be sent to the client at the end of this stage for final approval. Shots that are 1920 × 1080 are usually large enough to capture details for the client to discuss and mark up. Once all comments have been received then I progress to the next stage.

When I talk about the Refine stage people usually ask me why this stage is needed. My answer is multifaceted. One reason is that it helps in the pricing structure of a project.

Another is that clients need to be educated in design process. Refinements can take just as long as a design dependent on the client's comments. Usually I have minimal comments and can proceed with ease to the Deliver stage.

Deliver means exactly that. Materials collected and developed at the define stage should be close by for reference purposes.

The client may require large format renders or an animation. This will need to be created, formatted, post-produced and delivered on time. Usually I use online methods of electronic delivery.

Having explained my design process my number one piece of advice is to build detailed models (3.2).

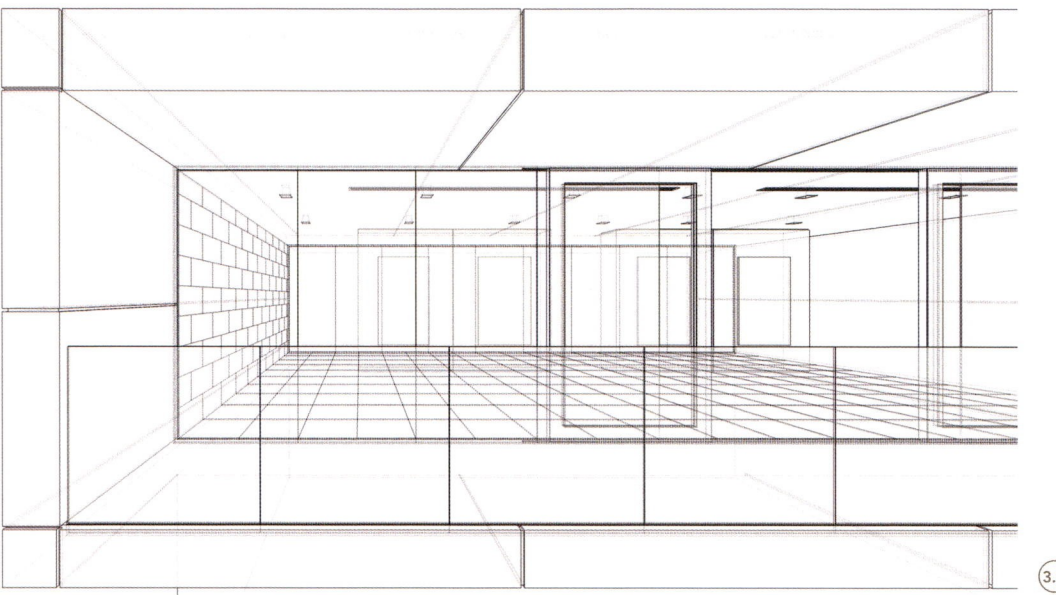

(3.2)

The more effort you put into detailing a scene the better the render results will be. The types of details I am referring to are things such as window frames, walls, skirting, lighting, switches etc.

If you simply apply a material to a plane and expect it to look like a realistic window, then you are in for a surprise.

The most common mistake and misconception I have witnessed to this day is that glazing is blue. Windows actually appear dark during the daytime. This is because they are transparent and allow light to pass through.

The second common mistake I see is a window with singular reflections. There really isn't much single glazing still around; double glazing gives you a slight double reflection adding to the realism of the project, so put two planes in your model (3.3) (3.4).

The reference on page 24 to external metal cladding is an incredibly important detail to bear in mind. Simply applying a cladding texture image to a surface will not produce the correct results (3.5) (3.6).

(3.3)

(3.4)

If you use the internet to search for cladding manufacturers such as Corus for example, their sites are full of specification sheets and technical drawings indicating how cladding systems are fixed to walls. If you make one standard block you should be able to populate your structure and add an incredibly increased depth to your scene.

Peripheral items are also important when you are intending to add an increased level of realism to your scenes. Items such as office furniture, lounge furniture, blinds, televisions and other accessories should be considered.

Modeling furniture and other items can be time consuming. If you perform a search on the internet you should find numerous furniture websites that have an architect's lounge or a supplier log-in area. These areas are full of 3D models, AutoCAD drawings and materials readily available for download. Simply insert them into your models and apply the required V-Ray materials.

3.5

3.6

 For more information on this topic, please visit WWW.FOCALPRESS. COM/CW/WYLDE!

(3.7)

(3.8)

(3.9)

(3.10)

Another pet hate of mine is looking at visuals that have little or no attention to detail when it comes to shapes and forms that intersect and connect. Standard details in the real world show us that where a floor connects with a wall there should be some level of finish in the form of skirting. So why not model the skirting details? (3.7) (3.8).

Where a ceiling connects with a wall why not show a shadow gap? If you model a ceiling with a perimeter shadow gap of 8 mm, then you will certainly emphasize the interior architecture and the clean details that make a space contemporary (3.9) (3.10).

Glazing systems have frames and their own unique details. There are many window manufacturers on the internet that show extruded aluminum details of a variety of styles of windows. If you create a standard 2D section of a window frame you can use SketchUp's follow me tool and create a detailed window frame in less than one minute (3.11) (3.12).

Lighting fixtures are equally as important. Including lights in your scene even though there are no artificial lights switched on during the daytime, for example. Modeling recessed light fixtures in the ceiling also adds to the overall perception of reality.

There are many resources online such as ERCO where not only can you download the actual light 3D model but the photometric web file in the form of an IES. I cover IES files in the Interior Evening section (Chapter 5) of this book.

Why are details like this so important? Well, if you have a design account to visualize an architect's design scheme, then you have to take into consideration that this piece of work will and can certainly portray a person's career, capabilities, ethos and dare I say it, the likelihood of obtaining future work. Therefore you owe it to your client to do a thorough job.

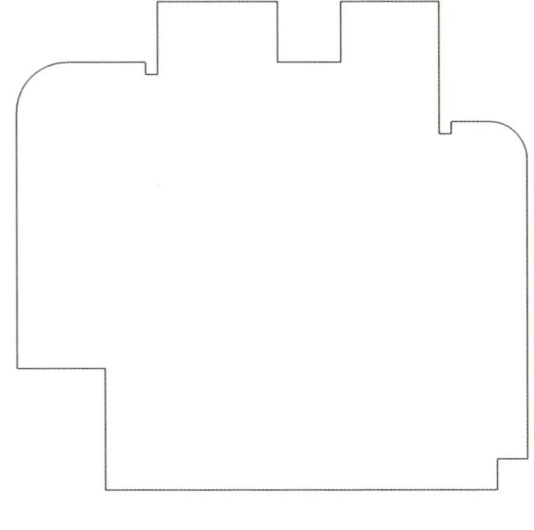

(3.11)

(3.12)

Planning and building a detailed scale model can take far too long in 3D Studio Max alone. I highly suggest using SketchUp wherever you can – as discussed on pages 16–17.

Once you are ready to insert your finalized model into 3D Studio Max you will be surprised to see that any components that you have created and any items that are instanced will also have the same properties within 3D Studio Max. Furthermore each material that you applied in SketchUp will also be brought into 3D Studio Max perfectly mapped and ready for lighting, texturing and rendering.

Let's go ahead and see the outcome of using SketchUp by carrying out this book's exercises.

CHAPTER 4

INTERIOR DAYTIME SCENES

DESIGN PROCESS

Interior designers face a tough challenge when creating visuals. Well, the fact that you are reading this book means that you want to pursue another avenue and create photorealistic renders.

The most important thing to bear in mind before you start any 3D assignment is that you must have a plan. When I say plan, I mean a key work stage plan. Make a cartoon set of what it is that you want to render. If you have been commissioned to create a set of visualizations, then creating a cartoon set will be one of the most valuable things you can produce. This will also help you break the process down into stages.

These stages require you to have the correct information to hand such as a set of as built drawings from an architect, or a set of concept sketches from an interior designer with indicative design direction contained within such as mood boards, reference materials etc.

As a designer I need to adhere to the most streamline work flow possible. I detest post-processing images. To me it is a waste of time, and time is money. I try and focus all my energy on creating a sterling scene that can be rendered from any camera position and produce great results. For this I use a method of lighting called IBL (image-based lighting).

IBL is an advanced method of lighting that is photographically captured to provide the artist with realistic accurate lighting levels from correctly exposed high resolution photographic images. These images are applied to a single light source created in 3D Studio Max and as such cast the high resolution photograph in a 360 degree direction throughout the entire scene.

This, however, is only a third of the work flow (lucky for you in this case its 50% as I have provided you with the scenes in 3D) as every scene requires a detailed 3D model and correctly calibrated set of cameras.

We will be using V-Ray Physical Cameras to give us the added control we require for our final renders.

V-Ray Physical Cameras are packed with real-world photography settings that enable us to manipulate the whole scene's look and feel.

Settings such as film speed (ISO), F-stop and shutter speed that are traditionally found within an SLR camera, make the features available in 3D Studio Max and V-Ray truly powerful.

It is a good idea to visit your local camera store and pick up a handful of digital camera brochures. These brochures usually contain example photographs and show the cameras' capabilities together with their respective picture settings. These can then be put into your scene as functional useable data.

It is essential to make sure that your scene is set up to utilize the extremely powerful tools available within 3D Studio Max and V-Ray. For example, if you are rendering a small room during the day with only one window, then you are going to find it difficult to capture any dramatic lighting. Alter the window structurally and the lighting will change immensely. This is the mindset you have to foster in order to push the boundaries of your capabilities.

In an effort to avoid creating the stereotypical, contemporary interior design visuals, I have reworked my original scene to encompass additional items that not only require technical ability to execute, but also require an eye for composition, color, material and photographic theory.

It would be incredibly easy to provide you with a scene complete with a polished concrete floor, a stylish sofa together with an exceedingly expensive lounge chair; however there are far more elements to understand and to consider when designing and visualizing interior spaces.

Interior daytime scenes can be tricky. If you take it upon yourself to Google image search 'interior visuals', you will be presented with a whole host of post-produced visual nightmares.

Although well composed and glossy as they are, unfortunately these images have undergone hours of post-production work. It is my ethos to work smart and not hard. I am not a fan of post-production and I try to reduce the amount in all of my work.

Using Photoshop to adjust every visual you create not only breaks the continuity and feel of a set of renders, but totally undermines and extends the overall design process.

I tend to find that designers and artists who have to spend hours post-processing images do not follow a design process from start to finish. With this is mind it is usually the case that most design processes are not followed due to fiscal and time restraints.

Going back to my design process; *define, design, refine* and *deliver*, key information is required at each stage in order to successfully complete the task at hand.

It goes without saying that defining the needs of the client is essential, otherwise how are you going to deliver and most importantly get paid?

In this particular case, for this exercise, there is not a brief; however I knew what theme and style I wanted to aim for and set about collecting information in the form of reference photographs of furniture and similar environments, materials and most importantly 2D and 3D resources.

Reference imagery is an ideal resource. If you have an image from the internet or a magazine that is a close match for the scene you want to create, then make sure it is always in front of you.

The minute you lose track of your creative direction utilizing these materials, and the minute you start reinventing the wheel, adjusting cameras, tweaking lighting etc, before you know it you will need to start your scene from the beginning in order to follow the strategic process that you developed! I have done this many times, it is an occupational hazard I'm afraid.

I find it imperative, whether you are a designer, digital artist or an enthusiast, to familiarize yourself with furniture brands, paint suppliers, materials suppliers and other interior design-related industry material manufacturers. Increasing your knowledge of real-world brands and products will strengthen your skills tenfold; it also helps you to remain relevant in an industry that is forever changing and undeniably competitive.

Why are my scenes different? Well, it is because what you see within them can actually be sourced in the real world. Why would I place a chair in a scene that cannot be sourced? If a client signs off on a set of visuals that you have created with that particular piece of furniture contained within it, then you have a problem and will have to find a similar piece later to specify and procure. In addition to this, why waste time

modeling it when you can download the actual manufacturers' models from their websites together with the textures and specifications? This comes back to the design process and being prepared. I always try and build myself a solid models library with textures that are available and once more procurable.

The same applies to things such as wooden flooring, textiles, carpets and artwork etc. Having these in place and ready to use will help to save you time during production, increases your professionalism and makes your work significantly noticeable and meaningful.

All materials and products have specifications that divulge a host of useful information for designers. Take white paint for example; you would assume that a V-Ray shader applied to an object would simply be given an RGB value of 255,255,255. This is fine; however why not actually reference the paint sample properly from a definitive source? There are hundreds of shades of white out there.

Take Ralph Lauren for example, although expensive and perhaps not what your client is looking for, they do have an incredible swatch of paints available for viewing on their website. The paint in this scene was taken from the site as a readily available swatch .jpeg for reference download. For me this is the equivalent to walking into a hardware store and leaving with a paint sample card.

In doing this I have lifted the scene and given it purpose and an increased level of realism. The paint also has a specification sheet, allowing you to see the properties of items such as light reflectance levels. This is key information that can be inputted into your materials palette which further emphasizes your skills and increases the quality of the final image.

The fundamental intent of this section is to open your minds to the alternative ways to use natural daylight and in turn realistically light your scenes. We will comprehensively cover real-world camera settings and how the combination of these settings and your scene can be manipulated to produce renders with depth and character.

This scene is extremely simple in terms of its form and composition. It is essentially a modern piece of micro-architecture in the form of a prefabricated living space. It has two walls and is predominantly glazed. Glazing is an extremely important aspect for interior renderings. It can be your best friend or it can be your arch enemy.

Ultimately the design of the space is down to the architect or interior designer. If you are rendering a room which has a glazed area of only 10 percent of the total surface area, then I guarantee your visuals are going to be pretty dark. This is the moment when some visualizers like to cheat. If you are replicating reality with physically based lighting, then what you see on your screen is an accurate representation of what will happen once the scheme is built in the real world, so don't cheat!

Depending on what stage in the design process this scheme is at, I would certainly suggest increasing the glazing ratio to accommodate as much natural light as possible. Often the architecture is fixed and change is impossible, so you have to be extremely creative in how you market the space visually.

Luckily we are going to be doing things properly and by doing so you will learn how to succeed with the most difficult of spaces to light without having to take shortcuts. Let's begin this exercise.

LIGHTING

The main method of lighting we are going to use in this exercise is known as HDR lighting. It is without doubt one of the most effective lighting methods to use when creating architectural and interior visuals.

HDR is an acronym for high dynamic range. What does this mean and why is it so relevant to what we are aiming to achieve? It is a term commonly associated with photography. It is a method of capturing an image and storing all the lighting information from the darkest points to the lightest points of the photograph, or exposures for those of you who are knowledgeable photographers.

The method of capturing these files is also referred to as bracketing. HDRI files have the file extension .hdr and are typically large files taking up storage space of up to and often beyond 200 MB. I cover all of the detailed topics about HDRI in the Photography section of this book (Chapter 10).

Utilizing these files means we can manipulate the stored lighting information and apply it to our scene. We can then adjust the intensity of the HDRI file to create a number of different moods dependent on the choice of camera settings.

There are other methods of lighting interior scenes. These alternative methods utilize the built-in V-Ray lights to replicate lighting levels artificially. I try not to do this because I want my scenes to be organic and have an increased depth to them. I do however cover alternative lighting methods other than HDRI in this book to balance out the argument.

For me HDRI files have multifaceted benefits. Like conventional photography you can shoot scenes anywhere in the world and they are yours. You can also purchase them online if you do not have the time or equipment to go out and create the perfect lighting files.

 For more information on this topic, please visit
WWW.FOCALPRESS.COM/CW/WYLDE!

The way in which these lighting files operate in this particular scene is not only to act as a backdrop to the scene, but also as an emitter casting beautiful pre-captured color and tones onto the scene's geometry.

The variable intensity of the light source enables surface materials to perform in a way that would be comparable to reality, absorbing warm and cold temperatures, displaying correct reflections and casting atmospheric shadows and bouncing color between multiple surfaces.

In our scene we are going to be using a V-Ray Dome Light. That is all. This sounds rather simple; however there is a considerable amount of work involved.

The V-Ray Dome Light will act as a 360 degree reposi-tionable backdrop to our scene casting all the pre-captured lighting information in a realistic way.

Let's begin by opening the file **04_Interior_Day_Start.max** from the project directory (4.1).

As you can see this is a pretty simple scene. The first thing we need to do is to let 3D Studio Max know that we do not want to use the standard scanline renderer but instead to use V-Ray's.

Open your render settings dialog by pressing F10. This menu can also be found by going to the Rendering menu and selecting Render Setup (4.2) .

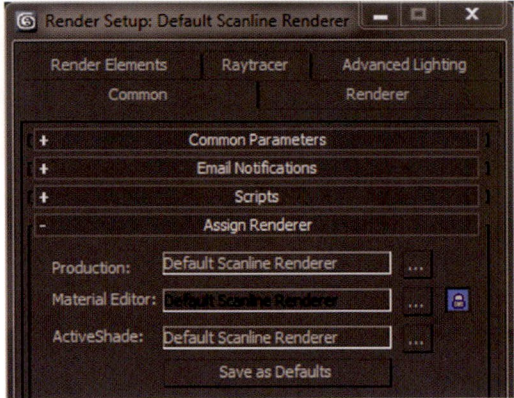

(4.3)

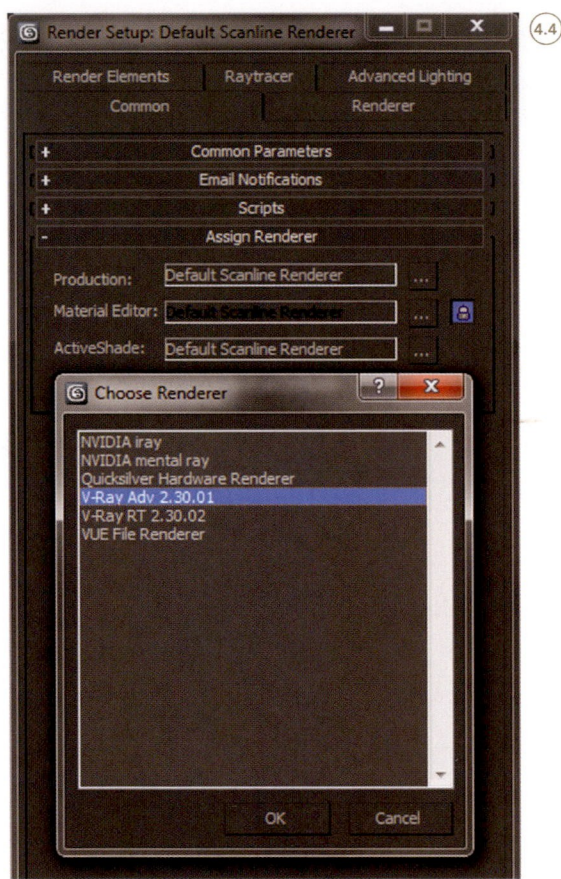

(4.4)

In the F10 dialog box (floating menu) scroll down to the Assign Renderer rollout. In the Production optional rollout press the ... button (4.3).

Choose V-Ray Adv from the pop up window and press OK (4.4).

If you are always going to be using V-Ray as your primary render engine you can go ahead and press the Save as Defaults button. This will enable V-Ray as your renderer every time you open 3D Studio Max.

Now we need to set up our V-Ray lighting system. Navigate your way over to the right-hand side tools palette. This is where the brains of the operation are located. In the Create panel, select Lights from the icons, it should be the third from the left (4.5).

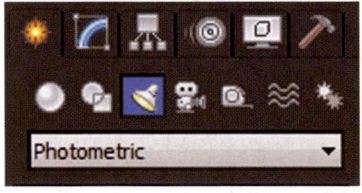

(4.5)

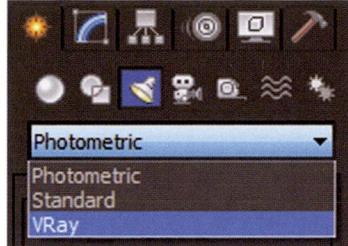

(4.6)

(4.7)

(4.9)

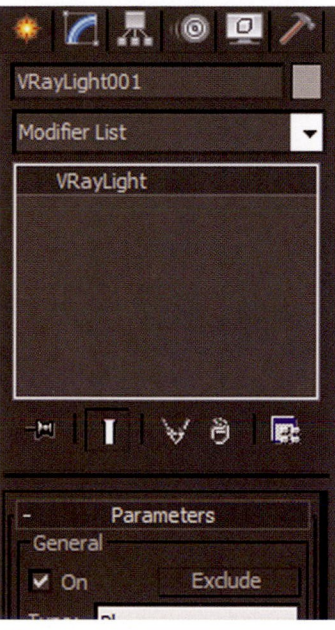

(4.8)

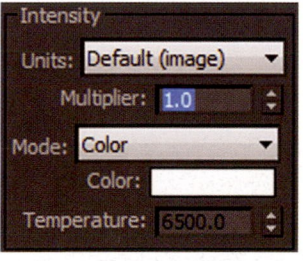

(4.10)

When you have selected this, you should be presented with another series of rollouts. Sorry but Max is full of rollouts so you will have to get used to it! Photometric should be first on the drop down list. Click this to reveal the rest of the options from the drop down menu. Choose VRay at the bottom (4.6).

A new and rather intense-looking lighting panel should have loaded with four options for creating V-Ray lights. We want to create a VRayLight (4.7).

Click VRayLight and then click anywhere in your scene within the top viewport. It does not matter where you place the light; it has no relevance with regard to the final rendered image. Simply think of it as an icon.

Now with the light selected we need to adjust the properties of the light. From the standard 3D Studio Max menu on the right click on the Modify icon (4.8).

In the Parameters section under General, switch the Type to Dome from the drop down list (4.9).

In doing this we are instructing the light to act differently in terms of its method of distribution.

Further down you should see the Intensity section. In here keep the Units set to Default (image). Also keep the Multiplier set to a value of 1.0 (4.10).

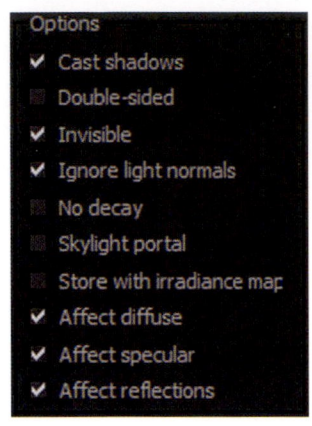

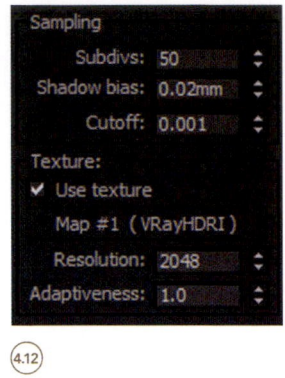

Scroll down to the Options section. In here are all the attributes that dictate the behavior of the light. We want the light to cast shadows so enable Cast Shadows. Leave Double-sided unchecked.

Make sure that the Invisible box is enabled. I will explain this later when we import our light source HDRI file. Here is an overview of what should and should not be enabled .

Navigate your way down to the next group of settings called Sampling. These are incredibly important. I receive a lot of inquiries through my website from artists asking why their scenes look so patchy when rendering with HDRI files. The usual rationale is that the light source's subdivision's value is not set high enough. If not this then it is a combination of the Subdivs and source resolution value of the HDRI in

the Texture settings not being set up correctly. Some people leave these settings low to try and achieve a lower render time, but unfortunately produce images with a vast amount of noise within them.

In the Texture options settings enable the Use Texture function. With this selected we are instructing the light to emit not just a color but to emit a texture. In this case it will be our HDRI file. Insert a value of 50 in the Subdivs section. This value can go up to a limit of 1000. I suggest not going more than 100. It can significantly affect the render time of the final image.

Set the Resolution to 2048, which is the highest value you can go to. Some people may say this is insane, it will take forever to render. Well, those people may only be using one HDRI file in their scene to emit light which is 200 MB. In this case I would agree and lower the value, but we are actually going to be utilizing two HDRI files. We return to this in a short while. For now make sure your settings resemble this .

Just underneath the Texture Options is another small group of settings labeled Dome Light Options. This is often overlooked and makes a world of difference when the settings are adjusted. If this is not enabled when we come to render we will see a large horizontal line below which all will appear black. More importantly we will have zero light emission from below the horizon line. Enabling this means we are able to use the whole HDRI lighting file instead of just 50 percent of it. Here is an example of not utilizing this option (4.13).

So with this make sure Spherical (full dome) is enabled.

The most important part of this process comes now. The lighting files I have provided you with have been prepared to expedite the rendering process.

Open your materials browser by pressing M on your keyboard. If your Materials Editor appears as the annoying new Slate mode, and in fact you are rather partial to being old school, then you can change back to the standard stacked Materials Editor by going to the menu at the top and navigating to Rendering, then choosing Materials Editor and choosing Compact Materials Editor.

(4.13)

Your Materials Editor may also be only showing 6 materials to play with. Keep pressing X on your keyboard and it will cycle through 18 materials and finally 24 materials. This helps with scenes that have the requirement for vast amounts of materials and shaders.

Now we need to import our HDRI files into the Materials Editor. Choose a blank material and select the Get Material icon (4.14).

The Materials/Map browser should pop up. Within here scroll down to the Maps section and select the Standard from the subsection. Scroll down to the VRayHDRI slot and double click it. It will load a small black box into your Materials Editor slot (4.15).

In the Materials Editor you will see a V-Ray Power Shader has loaded. This shader is wonderful; it enables us to alter the HDRI files from one location.

Where it reads bitmap: click the Browse button and go to the 04_Interior_Daytime project folder and within here select the Maps folder (4.16).

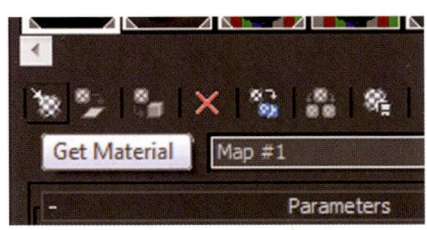

 4.14

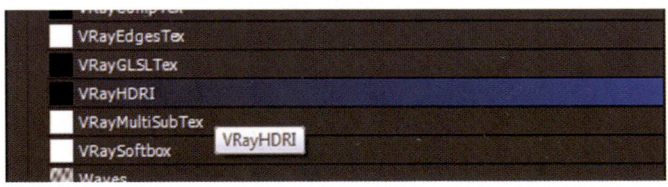

 4.15

 4.16

In the Maps folder is a HDRI folder. Contained within this folder are two HDRI files. I mentioned above that some people use only one HDRI file and apply it to their scene. We will be utilizing two files for two reasons.

First, one HDRI is for the background which will be rendered in the final scene, and as such the quality of the image needs to be rather high, otherwise there will be a large contrasting quality issue between our rendered geometry and the background image. The quality of reflections in objects can be seen also, so we need to make sure that the reflections are accurate and proportional to the scene's scale.

Second, using this high-quality HDRI file as the light emitter will significantly increase the render time. So instead we will use a slightly blurred version of the file at a reduced resolution. This also gives us incredibly soft shadows which will add an increasing level of realism to the scene.

Once the HDRI has been loaded, you will see a small preview in your Materials Editor. It will also look distorted. Don't panic as we will be dictating the mapping method in order for it to function properly.

A HDRI file is a spherical image that has been captured through dozens of bracketed photographs, and compiled into one large file. We need to tell the Materials Editor that this is a spherical image so that it casts light and shadows accurately.

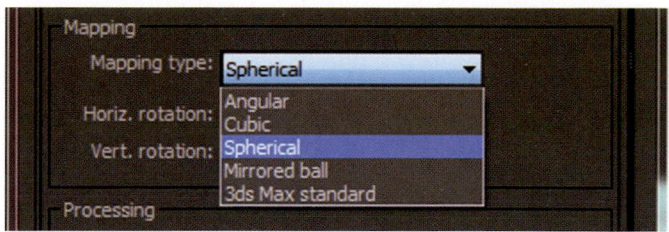

4.17

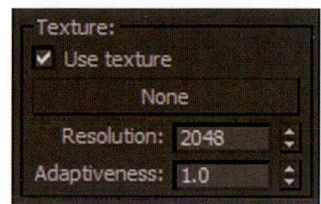

4.18

In the Mapping options select the drop down menu which will say Angular. Choose Spherical from the list. Now your preview looks better. Leave everything else as it is for now 4.17 .

We now need to instruct our VRayDome light to emit our HDRI file. Select the VRayDome light and navigate to the Lights properties. In here scroll down to the Texture options section 4.18 .

Very simply we are going to drag the HDRI material from the Materials Editor and drop it into the Texture Slot within the Lights properties. Like this 4.19 :

When the Instance (Copy) Map pop up menu appears you need to select Instance and press OK. This is important because any changes you make to the HDRI in the Materials Editor will automatically be updated rather than having to drag and drop the HDRI into the Lights properties again and again (4.20) .

Now we need to load the large HDRI file into our scene to act as the visible background image.

As before select a blank material and import the large HDRI file from the same location. Make sure the Mapping Type is set to Spherical.

A final important part in this step is instructing Max to use this HDRI as a visible backdrop. Press 8 on your keyboard to open the Environment and Effects dialog.

Under the Common Parameters section you will see Background. Check the Use Map to enable the texture roll-out slot. Now simply drag and drop the high-quality HDRI file from the Materials Editor to that of the Environment Map slot (4.21) .

Again when the Instance (Copy) Map pop up menu appears, be sure to select Instance.

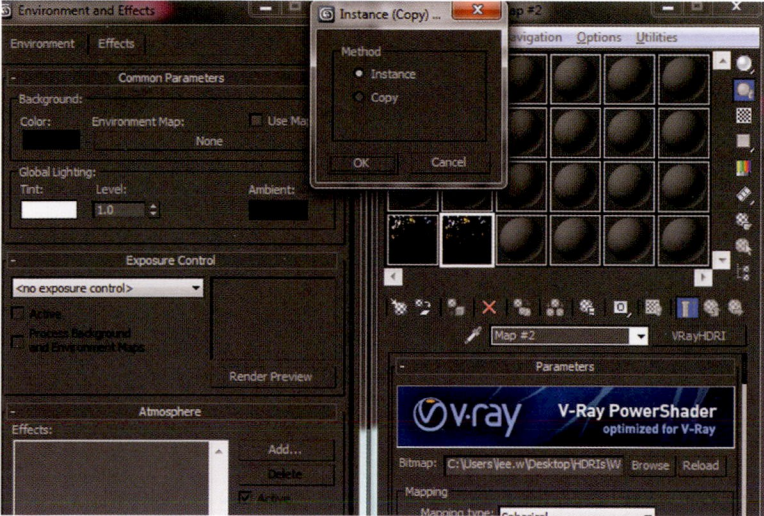

(4.21)

We have now created what is known as the environment light, the HDRI background and the HDRI mapped VRayDome light.

Remember this chapter means nothing unless we create a camera that can balance all of the lighting information we have created. Let's take a look at what steps we need to take in order to finalize this exercise.

CAMERAS

We now have our lighting rig set up. This will be useless to us unless we combine the scene with real-world camera values (4.22).

As daunting as digital SLR cameras are, they are actually incredible machines. They certainly contributed to my understanding of how light works. The same understanding once mastered can be put to use within 3D Studio Max using V-Ray.

In the resources section of this book I have added ideal camera settings for a whole range of environments. I have also added a full explanation of each camera setting contained within a VRay Physical Camera. So as not to go off track we will keep this section relevant to the exercise.

Now within Max there are a set of standard Cameras, a Target Camera and a Free Camera. Some people do use these when rendering with V-Ray. Most commonly they are used with alternative methods to HDRI lighting. As I mentioned before, some people use standard V-Ray lights in an artificial way to mimic an environment and they will be forever changing light settings. The more lights that there are in their scenes the more work they have changing the values to achieve a thorough look and feel.

Here we want to be able to control a range of lighting elements though the camera only. We do not want to be adjusting the VRay Dome Light. In reality we cannot adjust the sun so why do it here? We have to master the SLR Camera and its capabilities in order to deliver.

For Interior Daytime scenes there are whole spectrums of camera settings to use depending on what type of look and feel you want to achieve.

(4.22)

If you have ever flicked through the pages of the *Architectural Digest* or any interiors magazine you will see beautifully lit interior scenes. Well, this is due to the photographer bringing top-notch lighting equipment and spending hours setting up the scene and obtaining the correct light levels. We however require a less involved approach.

Some common errors I see in most visuals are the views through glazed elements in interior scenes. Where some artists show the outside world perfectly in focus and a different contrast to the interior space, in reality the windows would actually produce a rather holy-looking glow due to a high exposure setting being used on the camera (4.23).

While there are numerous sunny places in the world, there are equally parts that are overcast and the climatic conditions can severely affect the lighting conditions in a room. Direct sunlight also affects the lighting conditions in an interior space.

I highly suggest researching digital SLR camera brands. Often on certain manufacturers' websites there are example photographs shot with the cameras, together with the camera settings that contributed to the final image. These are ideal for setting up your scenes. All of the scenes in this book have been based on my Cannon 450D (4.24).

For now let's run through the settings for this scene.

(4.24)

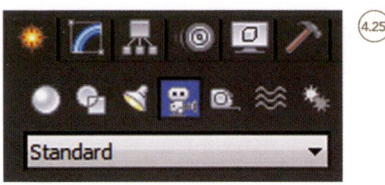

(4.25)

Open your scene from the previous stage.

Press T on your keyboard to go to the plan view of the model.

Within the create panel on the right-hand side go to Create and select Cameras. It should be the fourth icon from the left (4.25).

In the Object Type choose the VRayPhysicalCam button. In your top viewport go ahead and click the first point where you want your view to be taken from and second click where you want your view to point towards.

In the camera's Modification rollout you will yet again see an overwhelming list of modifiers. Fear not for we only want to alter a fraction of these. It is this group of settings that allows us to use real-world parameters to set up a virtual digital SLR Camera (4.26).

Under the Basic Parameters settings, maintain the selection of Still Cam as the type. Swiftly change the f-number to a value of 0.01. Next make sure that the White balance is set to Daylight. Finally set the Shutter speed to a value of 10 and the Film speed (ISO) to 600.0.

(4.26)

For more information on this topic, please visit WWW.FOCALPRESS. COM/CW/WYLDE!

Now we are ready to set up the main V-Ray render settings.

I have also included a detailed guide to all V-Ray settings on this book's companion website.

V-RAY SETTINGS

Are there universal render settings that are applicable to all types of renderings? The answer is no. All rendering settings require a fundamental knowledge of how they operate and will ultimately affect the scene's final output in terms of quality and time to render.

There are literally hundreds of combinations of render settings for V-Ray. I have included a cheat sheet paper for the closest render settings I find applicable for all the scenes on this book's companion website and for other scenes you may need to create in the future. I have also included an explanation of what each setting actually does.

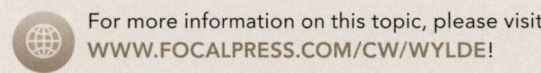
For more information on this topic, please visit
WWW.FOCALPRESS.COM/CW/WYLDE!

The main emphasis in this scene is quality. There are many materials in this scene where their properties require a certain selection of filtering in order to render properly.

Ultimately my intent is to have your scenes rendering as fast as possible without compromising the quality of the final image.

With your lighting and camera set up let us finalize the scene by inputting the sufficient settings.

Press F10 on your keyboard to open up the Render Setup dialog.

From the tabs at the top navigate yourself to the V-Ray tab (4.27).

Scroll down to the V-Ray:: Frame buffer selection area. In here we want to check that the Enable built-in Frame Buffer is enabled. Here is how this section should look (4.28).

Next scroll down to the next selection of settings labeled V-Ray:: Global switches. Under the subheading Lighting, make sure that Default lights are set to Off from the drop down menu. Also uncheck Hidden lights (4.29).

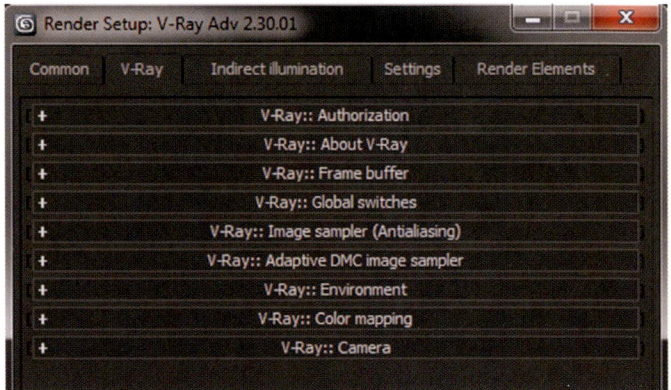

(4.27)

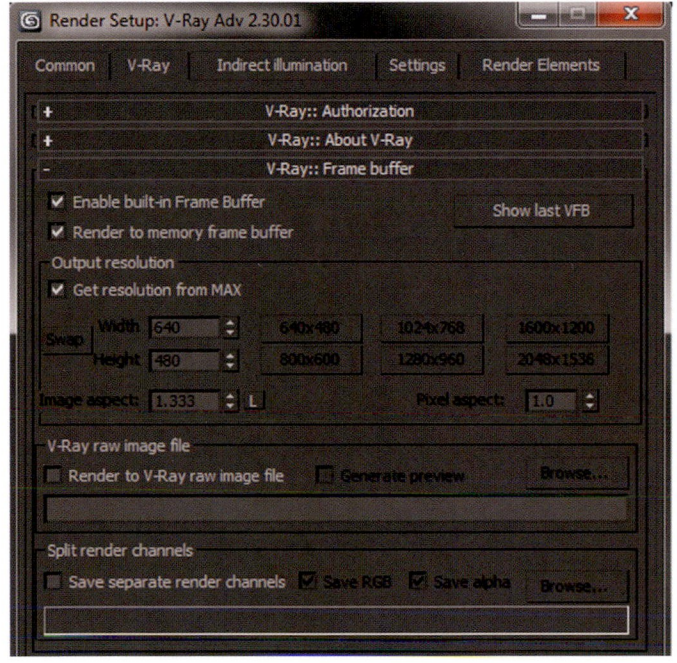

(4.28)

(4.29)

(4.30)

V-Ray:: Image sampler (Antialiasing) can be found, right, as our next collection of adjustable settings. This is incredibly important and value entered in here will determine the quality of the final image. In the Image sampler subsection, in the Type, select Adaptive DMC from the drop down menu.

In the Antialiasing filter subsection select Catmull-Rom from the drop down menu. Make sure that the checkbox is enabled (4.30).

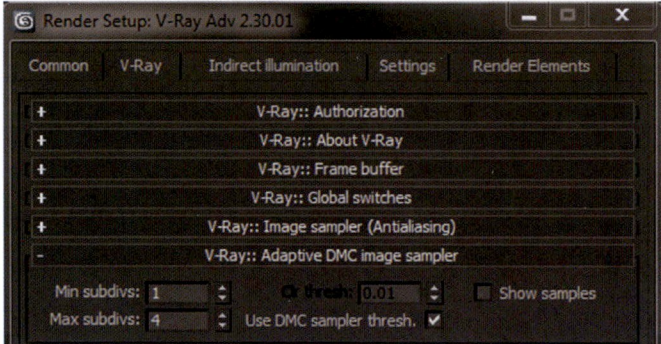

Now that you have finalized the Image sampler settings, you should find the V-Ray:: Adaptive DMC image sampler roll-out, left. Make sure your settings match these (4.31).

Perhaps one of the most frustrating parts of physically based lighting and rendering is when an image is rendered and displays burnt areas. This is because the HDRI files can hold a higher range of colors than can be displayed on screen (4.32).

We can avoid burning like this in the V-Ray:: Color mapping rollout. In here we want to set the type to Reinhard from the drop down menu.

I tend to find that the higher quality HDRI file I use, especially outdoor HDRIS that contain exceeding amounts of color information, require a very small burn value. In the Burn value input area, type in 0.015.

Over to the right, select Sub-pixel mapping and Affect background. I also like to clamp the output at level 1.0 (4.33).

Back to the top of the F10 render dialog box, the next tab along is the Indirect Illumination one (4.34).

These settings are also incredibly pivotal. We need to tell V-Ray how we want our scene's lighting to be calculated. From the V-Ray:: Indirect illumination (GI) rollout you will see that there are dozens more selectable options. The good news is we only have to change a few.

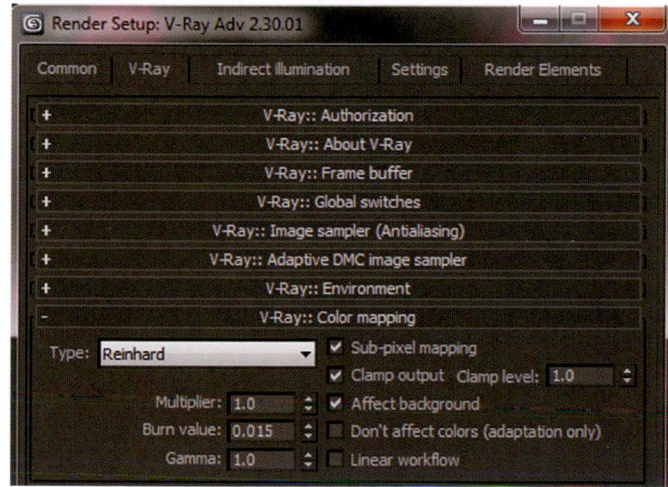

(4.33)

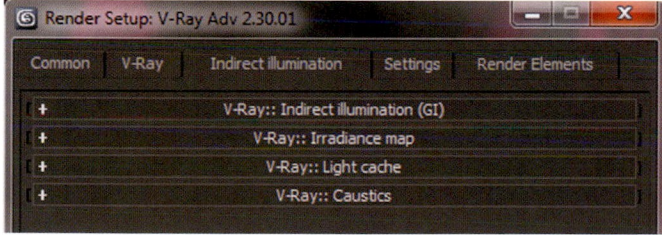

(4.34)

Make sure that the On checkbox is enabled. Below you should see a subsection named Primary bounces and Secondary bounces. Keep both multiplier values set to 1.0. In the Primary bounces GI engine drop down menu,

select Irradiance map. Now from the Secondary bounces GI engine drop down menu, select Light cache .

The following changes you are about to make will have a significant impact on how long your render takes to complete.

First, let's set up the V-Ray:: Irradiance map. A great tool that Chaos Group has built into V-Ray is the ability to choose a preset for the quality of the irradiance map. You can go ahead and select Medium from the drop down menu.

Just below you will see another group of settings under the heading Basic parameters, of which most have been locked. In here you should set the HSph.subdivs to 50 and the Interp.samples to 20.

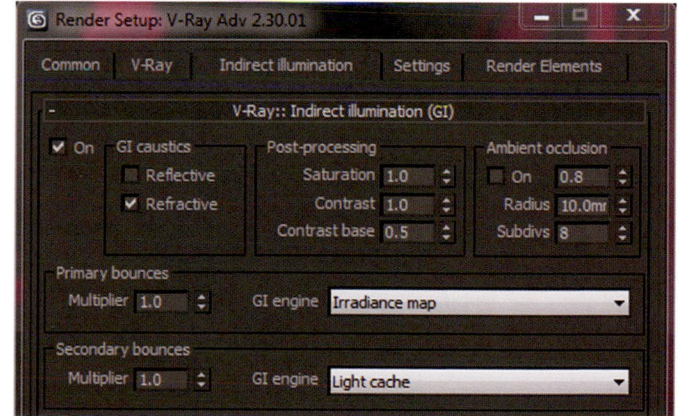

(4.35)

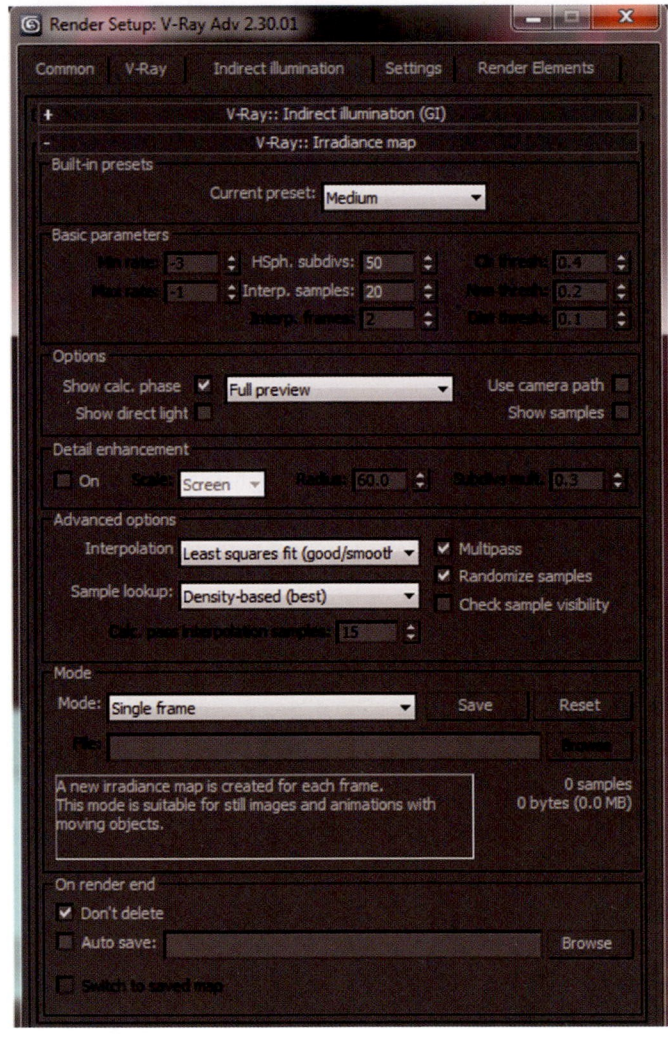

Just below in the Options area, simply enable the Show calc. phase. Here is how your settings should look at this point (4.36).

Almost there!

Go down to the V-Ray:: Light cache rollout. In here we need to make some small adjustments so that the quality of this task is executed within our scene.

In the calculation parameters area, enter a value of 1000 in the Subdivs. Make sure the Show calc. phase is checked as on. Here is what you should have at this point (4.37).

Now that you have the main render settings ready to go, all that is remaining is to set what size image you want to render. I usually like to render a high-quality image so that good details are visibly enhanced.

Press F10 on your keyboard to bring up the Render Setup dialog. In the Common tab scroll down to Output size. From the drop down menu choose HDTV. This will give you a canvas size of 1920 × 1080. I have personally printed A3 and even A2 presentations from this size output and they have been perfect for presentations.

Now you can go ahead and render your scene by pressing F9 on your keyboard.

The settings we went through and adjusted above (Irradiance map and Light cache) have now enabled you to view the

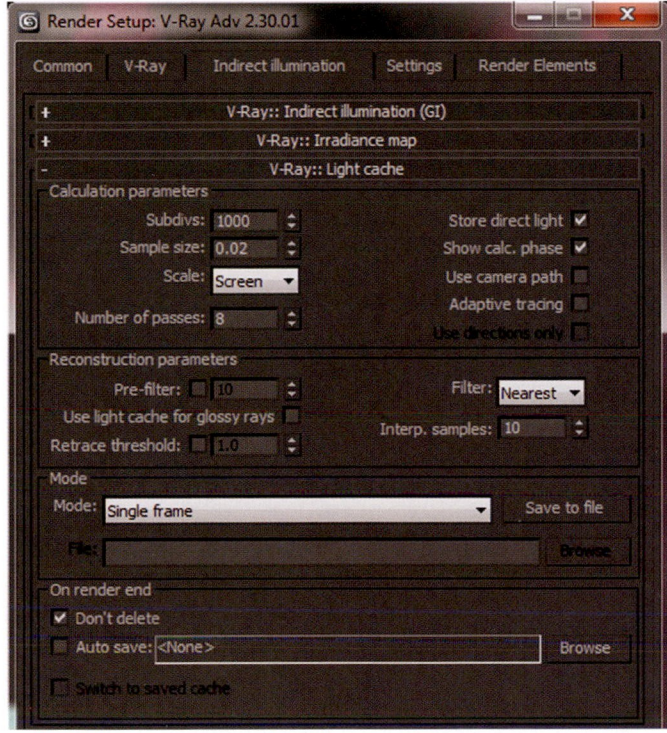

4.37

image being compiled in stages. This is a great tool as it helps you to see any errors that are in the scene without waiting for the final render; quite a difference compared to the good old days of scanline rendering.

RENDERING

Once you have completed a test render which should have taken around 20 minutes to render, depending on what type of machine you are using of course, you will notice that there is some room for improvement.

What you are seeing is an image that has depth and tone but is a little dark and could perhaps benefit further from an alternate alignment of background image and some minor adjustments to the camera's properties (4.38).

(4.38)

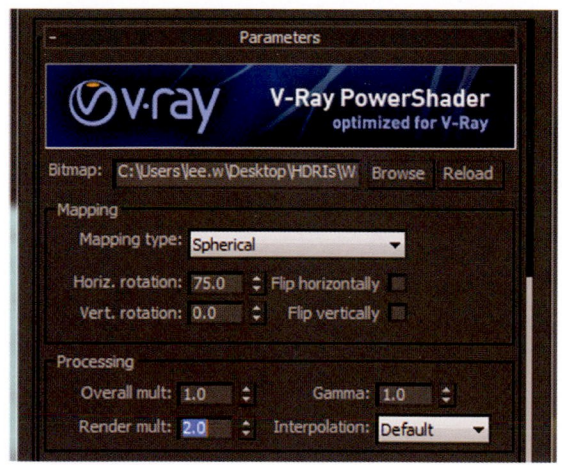

There are two workflow options we have available. We can either adjust the camera settings or we can adjust the HDRI settings to give us a more realistic feel to the scene. I am going to highlight both.

Let's start by changing the background HDRI settings. We can simply adjust the brightness of the VRay Dome Light source HDRI by increasing the render multiplier value to 2.0 (4.39).

Make sure that you have also changed the background HDRI setting to match. This should resemble your scene. Remember that you have two HDRIS inside your scene (4.40).

(4.41)

As mentioned previously in the lighting section, HDRI files are incredibly useful for changing the mood of a scene utilizing the same HDRI file. In this particular case we can see if the image would appear more realistic if it were in a shaded spot in the woods. With one simple numeric adjustment to the horizontal rotation value, we can change the dynamics of the whole scene.

In the HDRI material palette, you will see a group of properties under the subheading Mapping.

One important factor to keep in mind is that in 3D Studio Max the environment is a 360 degree world, if you will, just like ours in reality. HDRI files can span 360 degrees making them ideal for numeric adjustment to achieve alternate moods with the scene.

In the Horiz. rotation enter a value of 180. Do not forget to do the same in the background HDRI file also. Go ahead and produce a test render, F9 on your keyboard. Here is the result (4.41). Notice in this image we are presented with some

(4.42)

slight patchy elements on the floor in the form of noise. This can be due to dark areas in the HDRI file being cast onto the geometry in our scene that do not perform as well as other light areas of the HDRI. This is tolerable but I want to make sure that we have the best possible result. Also notice some scaling of trees and plants that seem too large in comparison to the objects in our scene. We can rotate the image out of sight to counter this.

In the Horiz. rotation, change the value to 75. Once more do not forget to do the same in the background HDRI file. Press F9 to produce a render. Here is the result (4.42).

This is a more suitable backdrop, providing us with an adequate amount of light to make the image look realistic. At a pixel size of 1000 × 563 this image should render in around 20 minutes (4.43).

(4.43)

Now that we have achieved a suitable image by adjusting all but the camera, we will now take a look at refining camera values instead.

In the real world if a photographer takes a picture and the image appears too dark or in fact too light, then a whole range of settings can be adjusted.

This alternative workflow is based on all the settings of the original file, where the HDRI Material values for both background and light source are set to a multiplier of 1.0.

In the Camera section I touched on the topic of realistic representation of views through windows in interior scenes and the realistic result that should be displayed (4.44).

We can achieve this in our scene by adjusting a number of settings. Select the VRay Physical Camera and open the settings menu on the right-hand side (4.45).

The f-number should be set to 3.5.

Further down set the shutter speed to 4.0.

4.44

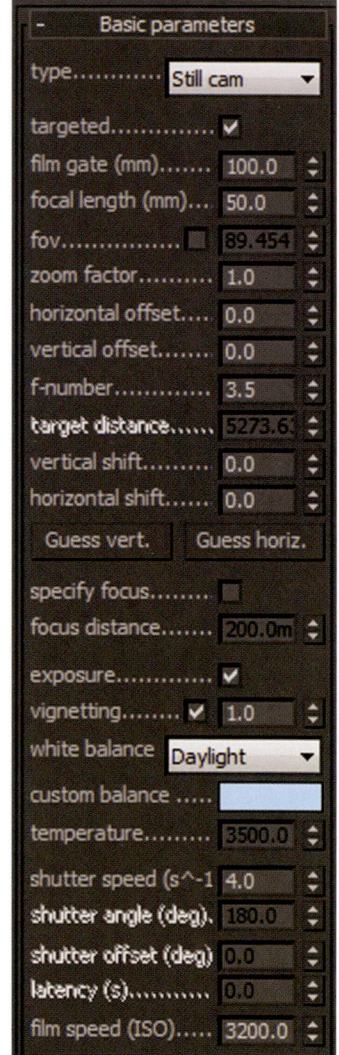

Just below this is the shutter speed (ISO) setting. Change this to 3200 and produce a test render.

In this render you can see significant noise around the perimeter of the room and a halo effect around the glazing areas. This is due to the camera settings, especially the ISO being set too high. Usually the higher this is the more grain you will see in the scene. We need to make some adjustments to maintain the lighting levels but increase the noise impact significantly.

Go ahead and adjust the camera settings to match the following.

This makes the render just about right for the setting that it is in. The lack of direct sunlight due to the scene being located in the woods would certainly bounce shades of green around

4.47

4.48

the room. The quality of the materials is much more prominent in this final render due to a higher f-number combined with a lower shutter speed 4.46.

It is entirely your choice whichever method you choose to adopt. There is no right way or wrong way in art. All that matters is the final result.

Finally, one more benefit in setting up your scenes utilizing the extreme versatility of HDRIS is that you can use these scenes for a range of other activities.

Take the image on the left for example 4.48.

Using the same scene I have made a copy of the original camera with the same settings. I have focused specifically on the table lamp and enabled depth of field. This gives additional realism to the scene and gives you more flexibility when focusing on key details without having to set up alternative files or having to Photoshop everything.

CHAPTER 5

INTERIOR EVENING SCENES

DESIGN PROCESS

Nighttime scenes and sunset scenes are without doubt my favorite to produce. They provide a platform to deliver dramatic lighting effects and can really transform a space into something quite unique.

The key focus when producing visuals for evening shots is to incorporate artificial lights to increase the level of reality through features such as highlights, reflections, and shadows.

IES lights are preset lights in 3D Studio Max that allow a profile to be loaded in to each light. These profiles or photometric data files, as they are commonly known, contain all the properties of real-world lights. We will cover IES lights in this section. These lights will be combined with the IBL method of lighting.

Not only do interior evening scenes require a significant amount of work to set up architecturally in terms of the 3D model, but they also demand the application of artificial lighting in great detail. Interior evening scenes also need rigorous planning in terms of materials in order to adhere to the design process.

Whenever I am asked to produce these types of scenes, one of my foremost thoughts is light. What type of light is required and where am I going to get it from?

V-Ray has a wonderful set of tools to utilize so that you can enter real-world values in the form of downloadable files from lighting manufacturers' websites. These files are known as IES files.

These IES lighting files are a standard lighting format containing what is known as photometric data. IES or Illuminating Engineering Society is the file extension we will be using for our exercise scene. We use these files to make sure the artificial lights in our scene are physically accurate.

I usually have IES files stored in my library which are split by manufacturer and performance type. You can find the specification for these lights contained within the manufacturer's website.

Attention to detail in surface materials is paramount in interior scenes. How do these materials absorb artificial light and not natural light? I do collect as many reference material images as I can and tend to show the client what type of look can be achieved upfront. This constitutes to positive working direction and once more defines your design direction.

There are two types of interior evening scenes. One is a scene that only contains artificial lighting and has no environmental light. The latter is a mixture of artificial light and natural light.

To maximize on the feel and depth of my scenes, I always try and render my evening shots during twilight. This aids in the overall lighting and most of all with the subtle reflections on the glazed elements, furniture and surface materials and so on.

There are many resources online from lighting manufacturers such as ERCO, Philips, AEL and more. I have included a list of resources on this book's companion website to help you develop your own libraries.

 For more information on this topic, please visit
WWW.FOCALPRESS.COM/CW/WYLDE!

When preparing a model for an evening render shot you have to make sure that you take the time to detail your model correctly. Simple textures that are applied to sheer surfaces will not suffice. There are many light sources directly and indirectly illuminating floor tiles, ceiling tiles, glass etc., so you need to adjust your workflow to maximize on the amount of detail in your scenes that will be emphasized.

When you think of wall tiles in a bathroom would you simply add a V-Ray shader to a plane? Would you feel that generating each wall tile with the correct mortar joint in between each tile would be too much? It is precisely these kinds of details that need to be upheld throughout your scene to add the level of realism you need to aim for.

One of the most significant benefits of using SketchUp to develop your base model is that elements like wall and floor tiles can be generated with relative ease, without the need for any special third-party plugins.

Bathroom scenes can be tedious. Balancing the light levels for a set of lights is something that needs to be worked out prior to opening 3D Studio Max. You must familiarize yourself with lighting levels for certain areas and how those lights should be performing.

Average illuminance information can be gathered from a variety of sources. There are different levels for different spaces; for example the average lux level for a kitchen is 50 lx, and for an office is 500 lx.

Normally a lighting consultant will have designed the space you are visualizing and you will have access to the lighting specification sheets and can simply input the data into Max.

Lighting does play a pivotal part in this scene as do the lighting fixtures. Although IES files are readily available for download, actual models of light fixtures are not that easy to come by.

A huge tip is to go old school. Make your own with the use of a template. I have added one for you in the scene, here is a section of how I model mine.

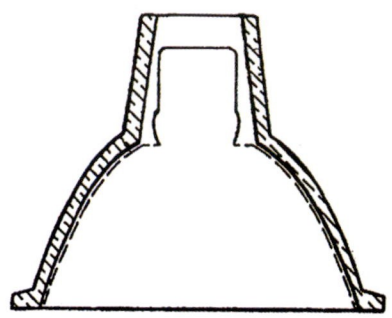

Applying the correct materials for the reflections in this light fixture will give you the creative edge you need for your images to stand out and be unique.

Putting the shape and form of the bathroom scene to one side, there are a number of peripheral elements that we require to complete the scene in a realistic way.

Bathroom furniture, sinks, taps and shower heads etc will all need sourcing. Sticking firmly with the ethos 'work smart, not hard', it is of high importance that you build yourself a library of sanitary fixtures. Why model a toilet? I have seen the worst visuals in the world with toilets and urinals that are not the right size, scale or even in the correct positions. There are literally thousands of suppliers on the web with products readily available for download. Start now and build your own library.

Finally this is a lifestyle shot, so the correct placement of the camera, its focal depth and settings will need to be planned. Build your scene around your view. I have witnessed this literally thousands of times, and in part have been guilty of it myself: getting carried away with your model. If you are not going to render it, then do not model it.

I have seen full buildings modeled with brickwork and stonework and beautiful details all for a partial interior shot! Hours and hours wasted that no one will ever see. If you can use your time wisely you can achieve truly professional results.

OK, enough life coaching, let's push on with the exercise.

LIGHTING

We are going to be using the two types of lighting as mentioned in the design process: a mixture of natural light and artificial light.

I prefer to use a HDRI file that has a mixture of blue mid tones combined with a warm setting sun. This acts as a subtle light source to our scene, highlighting glossy reflective surfaces and enabling a small amount of natural light to bounce around the room.

IES lights will be our detailed light source perfectly aligned with our ceiling-mounted light fixtures. These lights will directly illuminate the surfaces below creating accurate shadow projections enhancing detail throughout the scene.

One of the main performance benefits of using IES lights can be seen in the material reflections on solid surfaces such as aluminum, timber and porcelain. Overlapping reflections of IES lights and HDRI backdrops really does create unrivaled realism.

Let's start the exercise by loading in our HDRI backdrop image and primary environment lighting source.

Open up 05_Interior_Evening_Start.max

You have a completely textured scene complete with all necessary models and V-Ray shaders loaded.

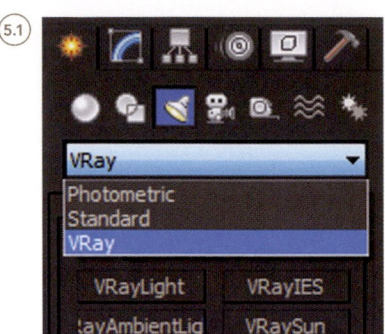

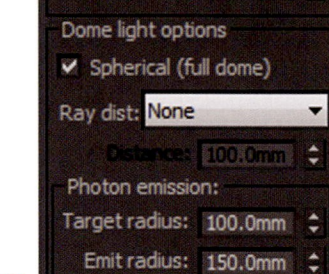

In the top viewport, T on your keyboard, go over to the Create panel and navigate your way to the lighting section (5.1).

From the drop down menu choose VRay.

You will now see that a new group of lights has loaded. From this selection you need to choose the VRayLight.

With this selected just underneath I would like you to change the Type to Dome and set the Multiplier to a value of 1.0.

Just a little further below, in the control panel, you will see the options section. Make sure your settings mimic these (5.2).

Finally we want to enable the Texture selection option ready to receive the evening HDRI file. Go ahead and enable the checkbox labeled Use texture. We want to also enable the light to cast 360 degree light so from the Dome light options, enable the Spherical (full dome) option. The settings should resemble the following (5.3).

You can now go ahead and click anywhere in your top viewport to place the Light source. Again it does not really matter where you place the light as it is environmental and as such will not affect shadow casting etc.

In this particular scene we are using an evening HDRI file as our subtle background light source. Here is a preview of the file (5.4):

Open your Materials Editor by pressing M on your keyboard.

(5.4)

We are going to load the first of two HDRI files which will act as the light casting source applied to the VRay dome light. Import a VRay HDRI shader into an active slot. Here's how (5.5).

With your VRay dome light selected, navigate your way to the Modify panel on the right-hand side of your screen. We want to apply this HDRI file to the Texture slot in the Lights environment settings. Drag and drop the HDRI preview image to the empty slot as per the follow image (5.6).

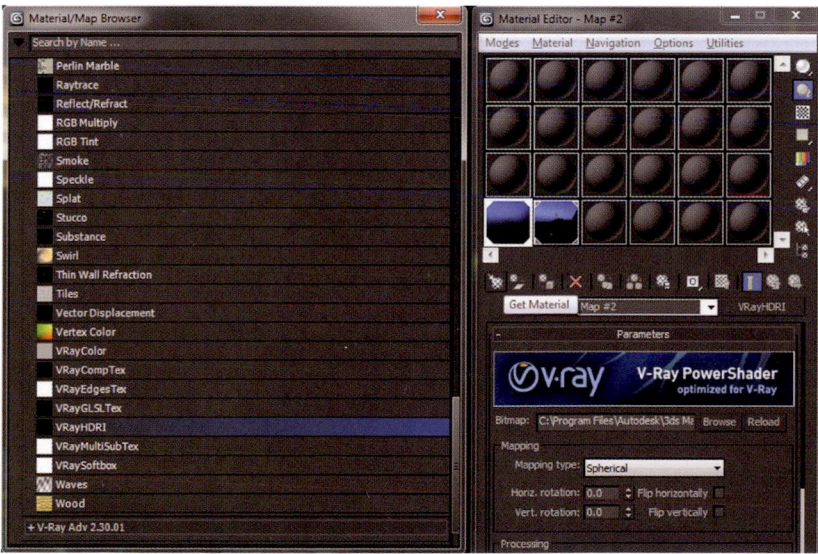

(5.5)

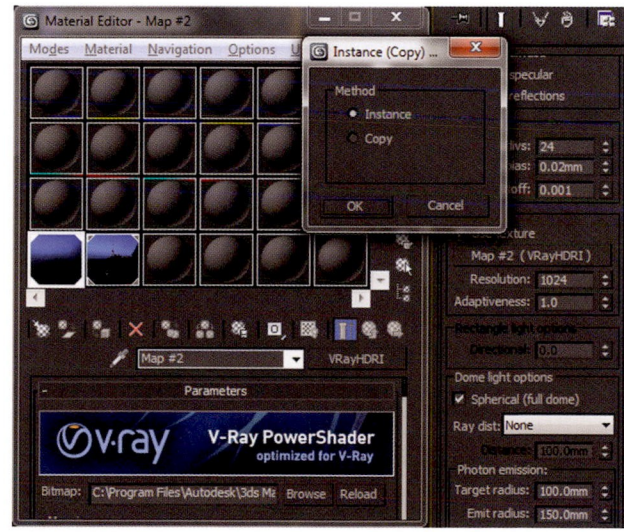

(5.6)

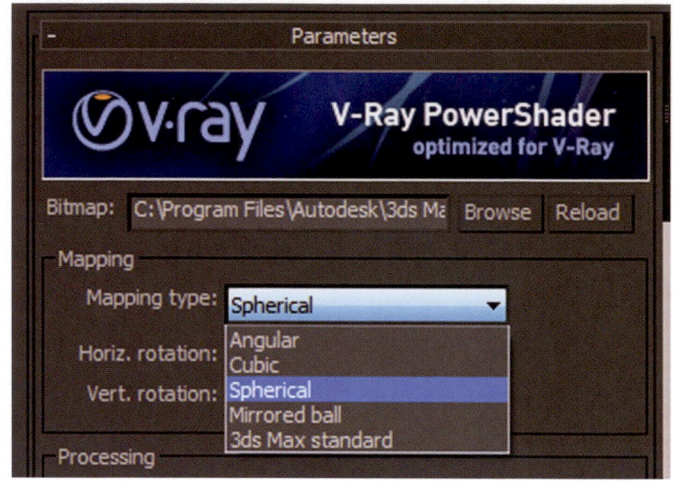

(5.7)

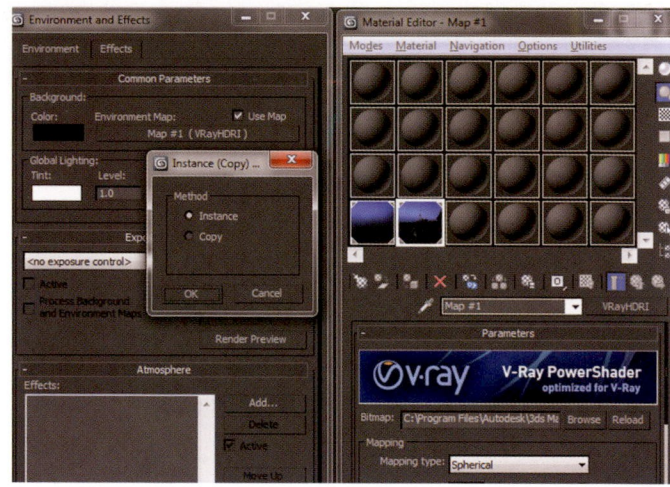

(5.8)

Now this is set up we can go ahead and load the remaining high-quality HDRI to act as the viewable evening background.

In an empty material slot go ahead and create another V-Ray HDRI shader and load the backdrop HDRI file into the empty slot. Make sure the Mapping type is set to Spherical as before. Your settings should resemble this (5.7).

Bring up the Environment and Effects dialog box by pressing 8 on your keyboard. We want to place the high-quality HDRI evening backdrop into the environment map slot (5.8).

At this point it is certainly a good time to save. We have the secondary lighting set up. I say secondary because the primary focus is on the artificial IES lights.

In the top viewport expand the view so that you can see the floor plan as large as possible. In this floor plan you will also see the ceiling detail and the main downlight positions (5.9).

We need to create a photometric light that will cast realistic light and shadows onto our scene's geometry.

The photometric light creation tools can be found in the Create panel. Choose VRay from the drop down menu and in the Object Type select the VRayIES button (5.10).

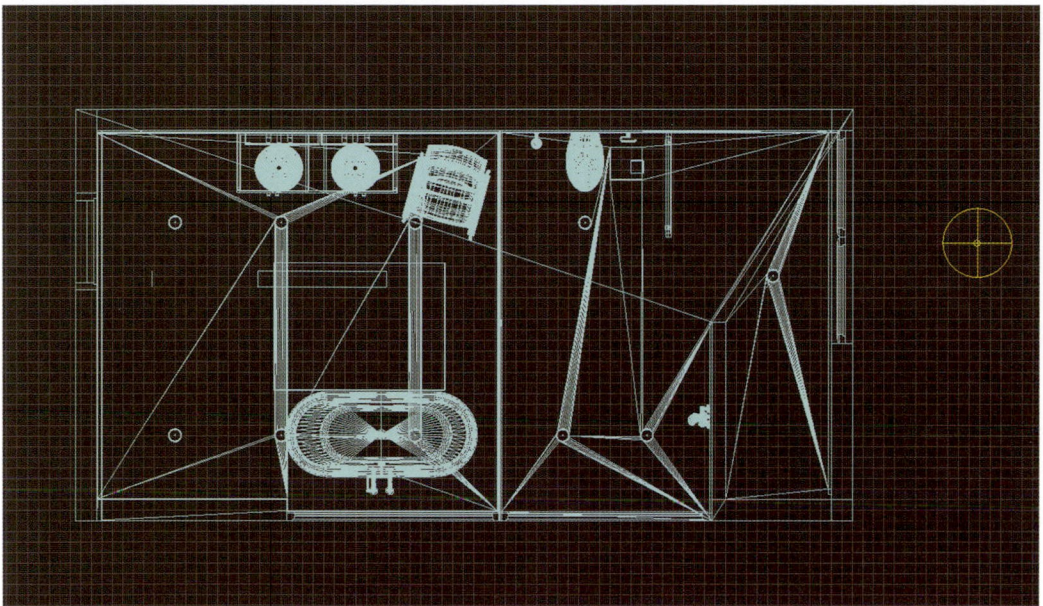

(5.9)

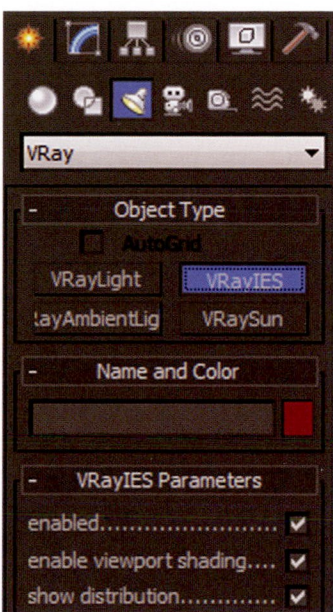

(5.10)

Creating a light source is simple, drag and point. The first click is where you want to place the light source and the second click is the light target point.

Try to align your lights correctly as per the ceiling layout. In the front and right viewport align the light vertically so that it points straight down. You will find a sample of my alignment overleaf (5.11).

The light source should be positioned and aligned correctly in the top and left viewports. Do not place the light source inside the light fixture, I know it seems logical because that is where the point of illumination is in reality, but in our scene it will simply cause dark circular shadows on the floor. Instead keep the source point around 10–15 mm from the ceiling in the Z direction.

Now we need to adjust the properties to match real-world values. Luckily the majority of these settings will come from the manufacturers' IES file.

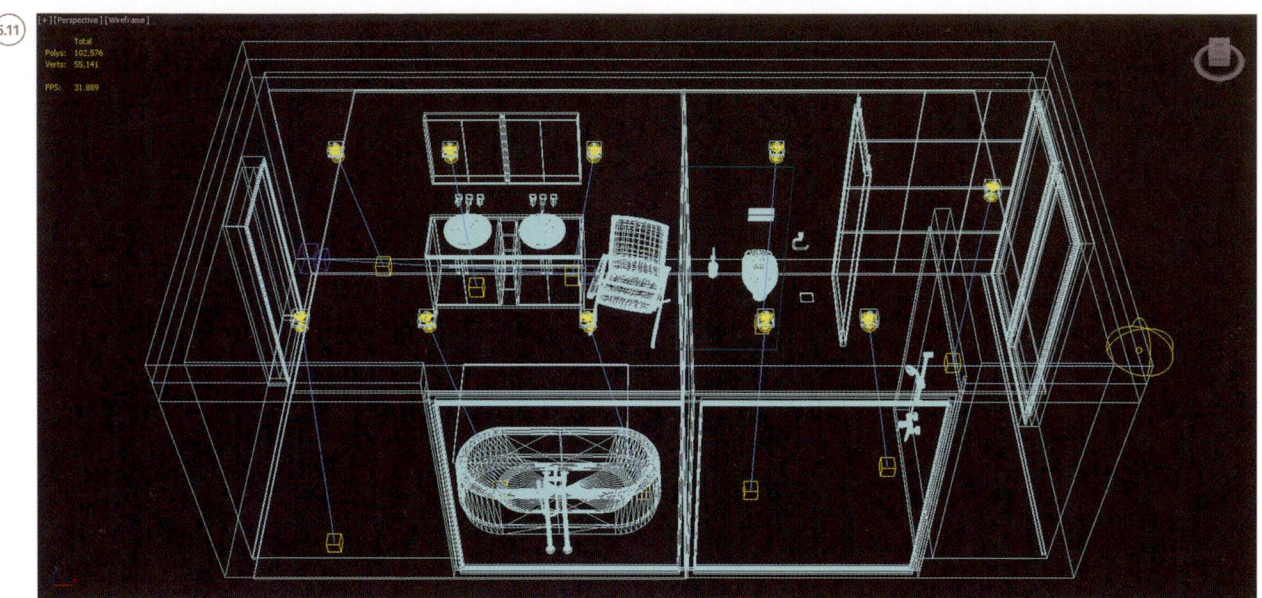

In the modify panel you will see a group of settings that allow us to significantly adjust the light. There is an empty slot with the name None. Go ahead and click this slot so we can load an IES file (5.12).

From the project folder load the IES file named 2782724. As soon as the file is loaded notice the emitter icon of your light change to match the settings of the loaded IES. This is reflecting the real-world light fixture attributes (5.13).

Now we have a master IES light source we need to copy this around the room and correctly align it to the remaining light fixtures. Be sure to instance copy the light otherwise you will

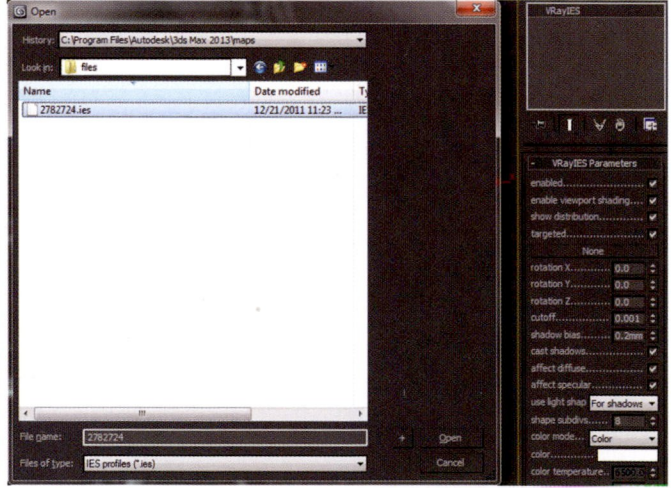

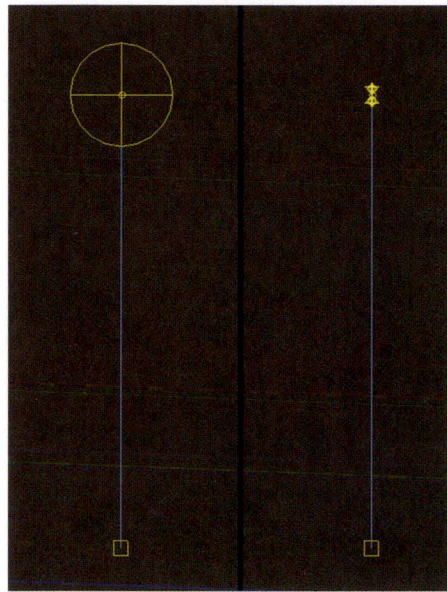

have to manually adjust every single light individually when making changes to brightness etc.

So that we are achieving a light level worthy of rendering go ahead and change the power value of the light to a value of 20,000.

Still in the IES light's properties menu, change the color mode to temperature. Finally set the color temperature value to a value of 5000.

Now we have the lights set up we can go ahead and set up the cameras.

CAMERAS

Calculating the correct settings for evening shots can be tedious. You must take into consideration the balance between natural light (what remains) and artificial light.

Having photography experience or understanding the basic functions of a digital SLR camera is certainly beneficial when using V-Ray Cameras.

Taking dramatic nighttime interior photographs can open your scene up to all sorts of alternative lifestyle shots for you to create.

In reality if you take a photograph in a dark room it is a dead cert that your camera will pop up the flash and flood the space with direct light, creating strong shadows and thus an overall dull image. This is far from what we want to achieve. As we do not have a flash we will manipulate the settings to increase and decrease the amount of light let in to the camera. The ISO value plays a particularly leading role in this. As mentioned before, the higher the ISO numeric value the higher the chances are of a resulting grainy picture, so we counter this by adding IES lights to our scene and adjusting the f-number and shutter speed 5.14 .

In this case we will be creating a camera set up for long exposures. For us this means the balance between shutter speed and f-number is an essential combination that we need to adequately gain control of.

(5.14)

Typically for nighttime shots we should be using an f-number setting of f11 and if needs be f16. However this may produce a darker image, but this can be balanced out by alternating the shutter speed value.

The main objective here is to achieve a realistic light level that highlights the detail within our scene and one that the client will ultimately be happy with.

Cinematography is something I research and keep up to date with as much as I can. It helps me to see alternative ways to shoot scenes and helps me to apply old and new techniques to my scenes. I highly recommend reading *Cinematography, Theory and Practice* by Blain Brown (Focal Press, 2011), as well as *Painting with Light* by John Alton (University of California Press, 2013).

These two fantastic books are filled with knowledge and years of practical experience shooting movies and lighting scenes. They have helped me to frame my scenes and use traditional physical toolsets in a virtual way.

One final element to this scene with regard to camera creation is depth of field. DOF is a byproduct of focusing the camera on one particular area of the scene. V-Ray Physical Cameras will act like real-world cameras and put a slight blur on the background while maintaining a sharp focus on the foreground and vice versa.

Let's go ahead and create the evening scene camera so that we can put all the above to practice.

From the Create panel on the right-hand side of the screen click the camera icon to reveal the creation choices.

From the drop down menu choose VRay.

Choose VRay physical camera from the creation options and place the camera in your scene.

Due to the nature of this space, its shape and form being inherently nondynamic, I suggest placing the camera at a slightly lower height and focusing the foreground on a furniture piece. Simply placing the camera in the middle of the room does nothing for the depth of the scene. We want to emphasize the beautiful outdoor twilight scene, so we need to place the camera over to the left. This also helps us to maximize the natural reflections combined with artificial shadows.

Now you have positioned your camera, let's input some basic settings so that we can go ahead and progress to the next step.

Select your camera and navigate your way to the Modify panel on the right-hand side of your screen.

In the Basic parameters section set the f-number value to 11.0 (5.15) .

Just below this group of options there is a button with the name Guess vertical shift. If you have the camera view set to your active viewport, keep watching while you press this button. Notice how all of the vertical lines in your scene are unified in the Z direction.

Another incredibly important feature to V-Ray Physical Cameras is the ability to set the white balance. White balance

(5.16)

is the process of removing unrealistic color casts so that objects which appear white in reality are rendered white in your image output.

Realistic camera white balance should take into account the type of scene you are rendering and the temperature of the background HDRI being cast onto the scene's geometry.

In this case we have a HDRI file of a dusk scene that contains mainly deep blues and some shades of white. As this is

the main light source for the environment, the white balance should be set to match. This is what I try and do for all my scenes; it significantly reduces the amount of post-production work that is required (5.16) .

In the white balance customization area you are presented with numerous options from the drop down menu, or you can enter a custom value. For this exercise select Daylight (5.17) .

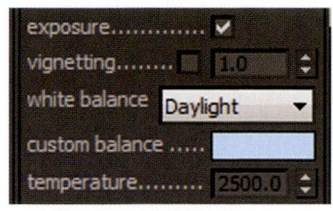 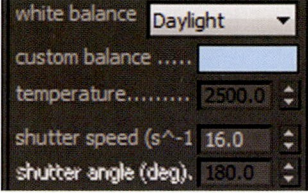

 (5.17) (5.18)

Underneath this option is the shutter speed. Change this value to 16.0 (5.18).

The ISO setting should be set to a value of 200.0. We can adjust this later when producing test renders.

Now we need to focus on the V-Ray system settings.

V-RAY SETTINGS

Interior evening render settings are similar to the interior daytime settings. There are however a few subtle changes we need to make to fully achieve our desired result.

In an effort to maintain the render times to complete within one hour, the V-Ray render settings will reflect this as will the quality of the final image.

Press F10 on your keyboard to open up the Render Setup dialog.

From the tabs at the top navigate yourself to the V-Ray tab (5.19).

Scroll down to the V-Ray:: Frame buffer selection area. In here we need to check that the Enable built-in Frame Buffer is enabled. Over the page is how this section should look (5.20).

Now scroll down to the next selection of settings labeled V-Ray:: Global switches. Under the subheading Lighting, make sure that Default Lights option is selected as being Off from the drop down menu. Also uncheck Hidden Lights (5.21).

V-Ray:: Image sampler (Antialiasing) can be found below as our next collection of adjustable settings. These are incredibly important and values entered within here will determine the quality of the final image. In the Image

CHAPTER FIVE

| 77

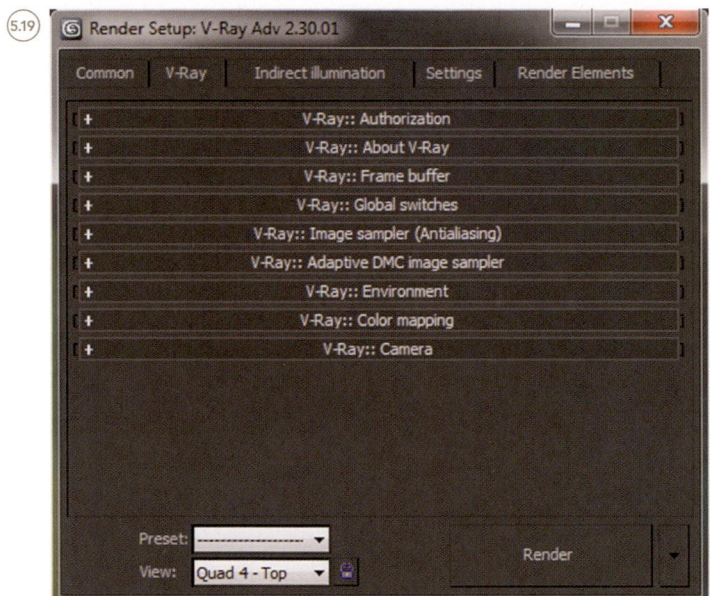

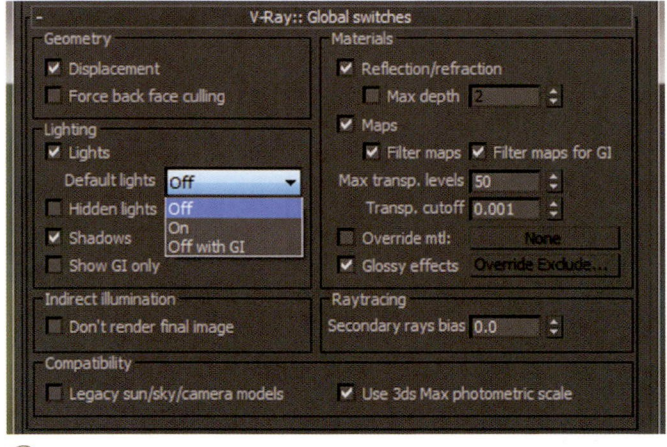

sampler subsection, in the Type, select Adaptive DMC from the drop down menu.

In the Antialiasing filter subsection select Catmull-rom from the drop down menu. Make sure that the checkbox is enabled as On (5.22).

Now you have finalized the Image sampler settings you should find the V-Ray:: Adaptive DMC image sampler roll-out just below. Make sure your settings match those shown (5.23).

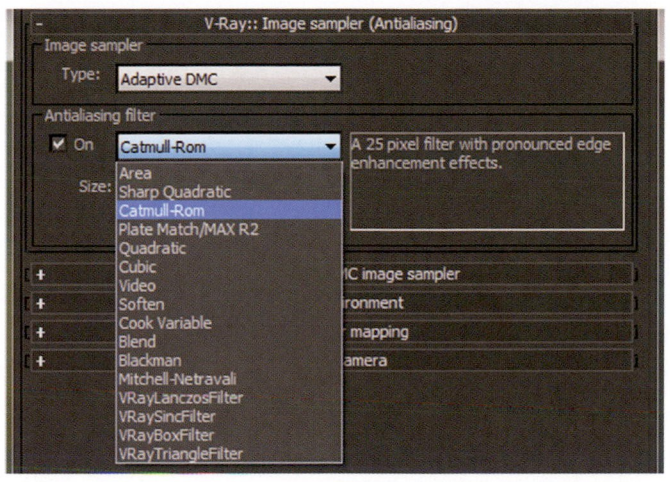

(5.22)

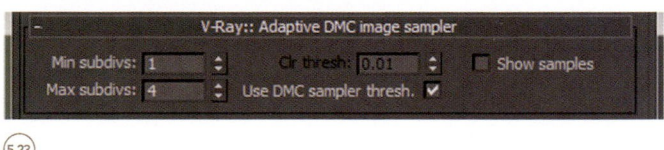

(5.23)

Perhaps one of the most frustrating parts of physically based lighting and rendering is when an image is finally rendered but displays burnt areas. This is because the HDRI files can hold a higher range of colors than can be displayed on screen and as such need controlling in order to become visible. These settings will also affect the performance of the IES file (5.24).

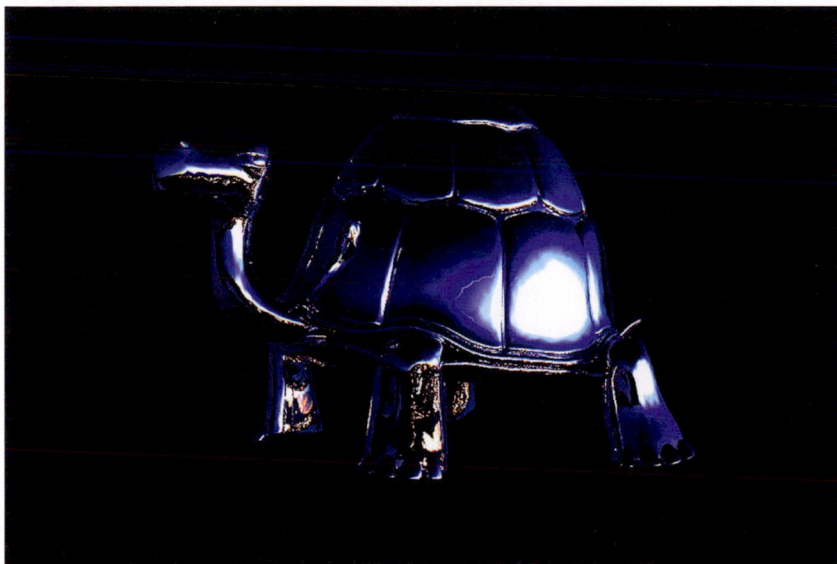

(5.24)

We can avoid burning in the V-Ray:: Color mapping rollout. In here we want to set the type to Reinhard from the drop down menu.

I tend to find that the higher quality HDRI file I use, especially outdoor HDRIS that contain tremendous amounts of color information, require a very small burn value. In the Burn value input area, type in 0.015. We can alter this to suit the IES performance later.

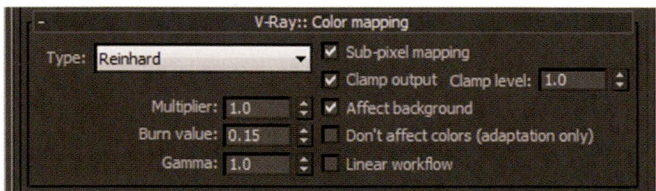

5.25

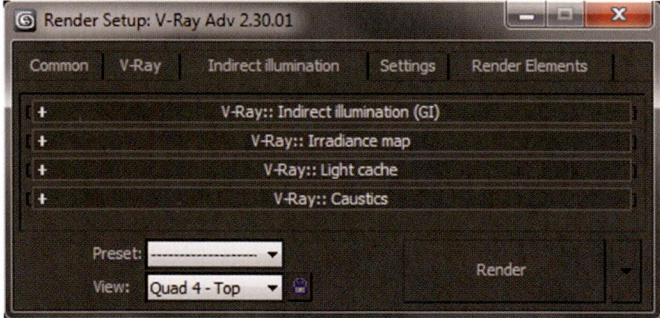

5.26

Over to the right, select Sub-pixel mapping and Affect background. I once more like to clamp the output at level 1.0 5.25 .

Back to the top of the F10 Render dialog box, the next folder along is the Indirect Illumination tab 5.26 .

These settings are also incredibly pivotal. We need to inform V-Ray how we want our scene to be calculated.

From the V-Ray:: Indirect illumination (GI) rollout you will see there are dozens of selectable options. The good news is we only have to change a few of these.

Make sure the On checkbox is enabled. Below you should see a subsection named Primary bounces and Secondary bounces.

Keep both multiplier values set to 1.0. In the Primary bounces GI engine drop down menu, select Irradiance map. Now from the Secondary bounces GI Engine drop down menu, select Light cache 5.27 .

The following changes you are about to make will also have a significant impact on how long your render takes to complete, bearing in mind you have multiple light sources.

First, let's set up the V-Ray:: Irradiance map. A great tool that Chaos Group has built into V-Ray is the ability to choose a preset for the quality of the irradiance map. You can go ahead and select Medium from the drop down menu.

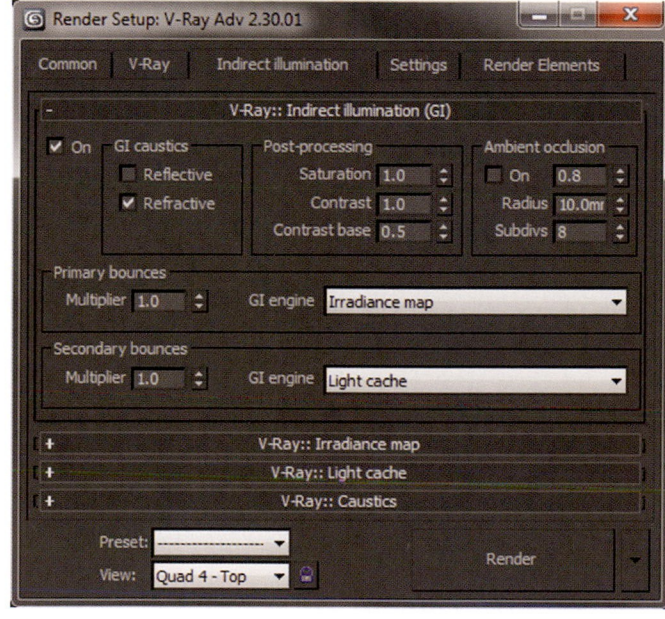

(5.27)

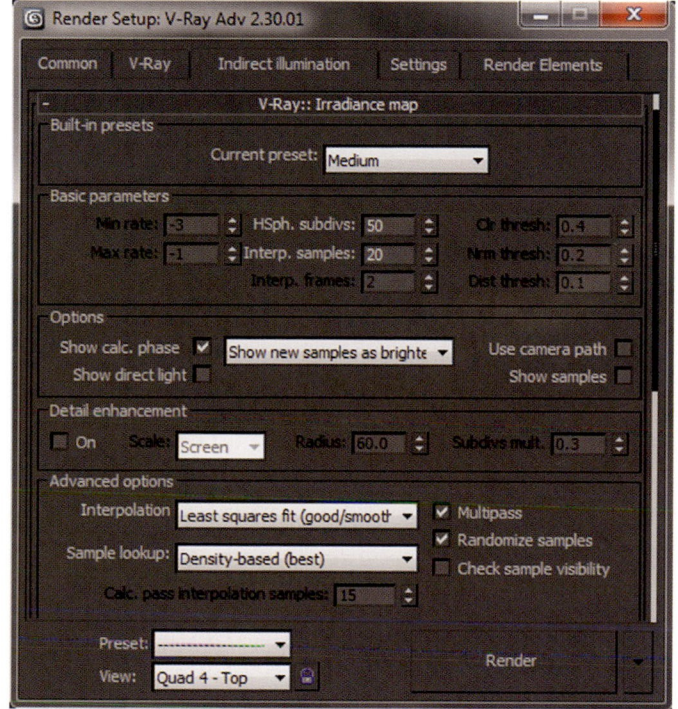

(5.28)

Just below you will see another range of settings under the heading Basic parameters, of which most have been locked.

In here you should set the HSph.subdivs to 50 and the Interp.samples to 20.

Just below in the Options area, simply enable the Show calc. phase. Here above right is how your settings should look at this point (5.28).

Almost there!

Go down to the V-Ray:: Light cache rollout. In here we need to make some minor adjustments so that the resulting quality of this task is resembled in our scene.

In the Calculation parameters area, enter a value of 1000 in the Subdivs. Make sure that the Show calc. phase is checked as on. Overleaf is what you should have at this point (5.29).

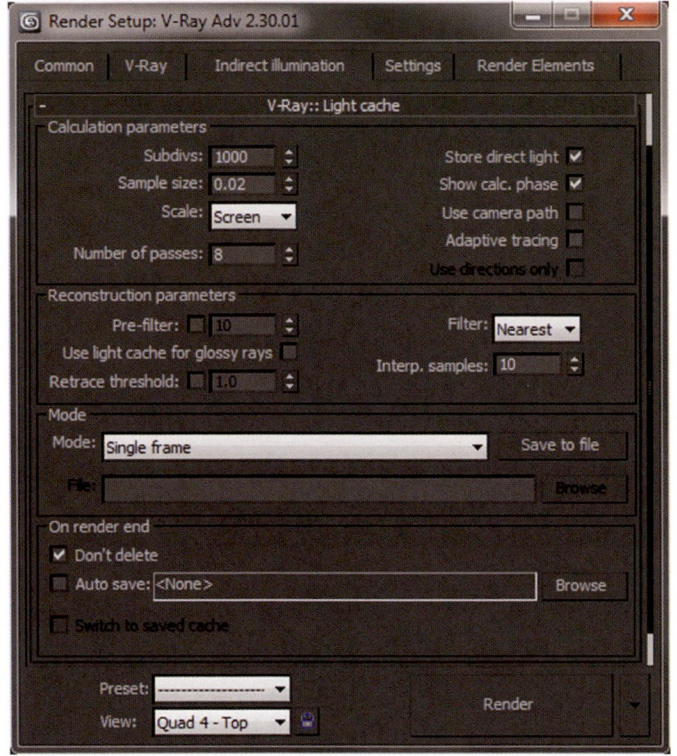

5.29

Now you have the main render settings ready to go, all that is remaining is to set the size of render output for your scene.

I usually like to render a decent quality image so that architectural details are enhanced.

Press F10 on your keyboard to bring up the Render Setup dialog.

In the Common tab scroll down to Output size settings.

From the drop down menu choose HDTV. This will give you a canvas size of 1920 × 1080. I have personally printed A3 and even A2 presentations from this size output and they have been perfect for presentations.

RENDERING

Refining the final stages of your project can be incredibly exciting and equally soul-destroying.

Fiddling and adjusting a multitude of settings can really stress out designers. Furthermore just keeping track of your changes is tricky unless you have the server space for 10+ variations of your scene.

Luckily you have me to spill the beans. Stay focused; it is an ideal time to bring out the reference images from the first stage of the project as your guide if you are working on your own projects in line with this exercise.

Now we are in a position to do so, let's go ahead and produce a test render by pressing F9 on your keyboard (5.30).

(5.30)

It is an average result; we do not want average so we have to make some minor adjustments in order to increase the color depth and feel of the scene.

In the VRay Physical Camera properties you can adjust the color temperature to a custom value to further match the background HDRI as previously mentioned.

We need to establish a neutral reference point to match the camera as naturally as possible. In this case it is the bluish twilight tones.

Color temperatures vary. Candlelight for example has a color temperature of 1000–2000 K. Clear sky on a sunny day has a color temperature of 3000–4000 K.

In our scene we want to aim for a temperature of around 6500–8000 K. This seems pretty broad; however we can adjust the value in integers of 100 to fine tune the camera to obtain the desired effect.

In scenes containing multiple illuminants with varied color temperatures, such as our IES lights for example, normally photographers can leave an automatic white balance on their camera and it will calculate an average white balance based on all lighting information in the scene.

We require additional control, because we want to emphasize the warm lights against the cool exterior HDRI light. For this we must enter our own values based on the neutral reference point.

Change the value in the white balance section of the camera settings to custom, and enter a value of 6500.

Execute another test render; it should only take 25 minutes assuming you have the DOF function temporarily switched off. Here is the result (5.31).

We can further improve the tone of the image through the lighting controls.

The IES files can also be adjusted to suit the scene. We want to emphasize the warmth of the artificial illumination so we need a value of around 2000–4000 K. Select one of the IES lights and change the color temperature to 2000. Execute a test render, F9 (5.32).

See how there is such a dramatic difference between the interior and exterior lighting? The result is nicely balanced but the realistic highlights from the artificial lights are not quite there yet.

There may be an occasion that justifies the adjustment of the IES power value. Sometimes directly importing an IES file without adjusting the power value can result in very dark scenes. In our scene I suggest increasing the power of the IES light to 30,000. You can view the result on page 86 (5.33).

The result remains nicely balanced but I am not content with it yet. Go ahead and ramp up the power value of your IES lights to 45,000.

5.31

5.32

 5.33

 5.34

Adjusting the IES power of an instanced light means we are uniformly adjusting the light levels throughout the whole scene. There may be an occasion when you only want the foreground lights to be a high power and the rest a lower power. This is an incredibly effective way of highlighting architectural details.

I am often asked the question, why is my scene so dark? I have seen IES lighting power values of up to 350,000 used.

This can be due to improper world scaling. Always make sure you work to a scale. Even if the SketchUp model is metric, you have to make sure that 3D Studio Max is set to metric also, otherwise your lighting scale will be ruined. I also try to make sure that the IES files I am collecting for use within my scenes are from professional, reputable lighting companies.

Again produce a test render by pressing F10 (5.34).

For me this still looks a little flat. The reason is perhaps that we have a too low level of color burn in our color mapping settings. We need to change this low amount and slightly decrease the effect.

Press F10 to open the Render settings dialog. Go to V-Ray in the tabs at the top of the pop up window.

Scroll down to the Color mapping section. In here change the Burn value from 0.15 to 0.3. Save your file. Press F9 to render your scene (5.35).

Now I am happy with the level of lighting contained. You may not be so happy so keep trying out the settings to see what results you get.

Finally we need to enable the depth of field camera function. Select your camera and open up the properties through the modify panel. Be warned, this will take longer to render.

Scroll down to the sampling settings. Once DOF is enabled change the Subdivs numeric value to 10.0.

The depth of field option is not essential but nonetheless adds realistic depth to the scene. The ethos of this book is to stray away from scientific jargon and remain practical, so with that in mind I will explain a simple way to work out how you should set your camera up to utilize DOF.

The depth of field is the distance in front and beyond an object that is in focus or you want to focus on. There are three main elements that affect DOF, the first being the size of the aperture, the second being the distance to the object and finally the lens you are using.

In terms of photography DOF can take a while to figure out given the above variables. In V-Ray we can keep this relatively simple in order to create rather interesting results.

The first thing is to figure out why you are using the DOF function. It should be to highlight a specific architectural, interior detail or product.

5.35

5.36

In your scene if you right click and select Unhide all from the quad menu you will see that a camera and a piece of geometry have appeared. Yes we are using Mr. Turtle again. He will be your primary focus object in the scene. The camera has the DOF function already enabled.

Now you can reposition the turtle in your scene and practice alternating the focal depth of your camera in order to see the results.

Here is the render output from the initial position. Remember that enabling the DOF function can increase render times significantly (5.36).

CHAPTER 6

INTERIOR MOCKUP SCENES

DESIGN PROCESS

Mockup scenes are an incredibly effective way of visualizing items such as furniture, products and partial scenes of a design in a simple and fast way.

I usually use these scenes for commercial furniture mockups. If you pick up a magazine such as *Harper's Bazaar*, *Wallpaper** or *World of Interiors* for example, you will see many adverts for furniture.

These photographs have been shot in a preconfigured studio lighting environment. Most of these shoots involve artificial light and some perhaps a small percentage of natural light.

Mockup scenes significantly reduce the need for any auxiliary modeling for the environment that they are in, what you see is what you get and you can create very impressive results dependent on your subject.

6.1

HDRI lighting plays a vital role in the lighting as its simplified workflow makes it easy to create realistic renders in short amounts of time.

For this scene I modeled the timber paneling in SketchUp which took around five minutes. There is nothing truly complicated about this scene.

Here is a snapshot of the model so that you can see the amount of minimal geometry involved (6.1).

Coming back to workflow, you will notice that there is no furniture in the SketchUp file. This is because the furniture I use has been acquired from the actual manufacturer. They normally make available 3D models in .3DS format or if you are lucky in .max on their websites.

Work smart not hard! Your scene then becomes a matter of suitable placement of furniture and artwork in order to make it look real.

I tend to find that the more interesting HDRI files you have of interior and exterior spaces, the more diversity you can offer utilizing just a single .max lighting rig. Here is the HDRI file I used for this scene (6.2).

(6.2)

What I particularly like about these types of scenes is that with a few small changes to the materials and the HDRI file, you can have what looks like a total different scene, so the flexibility is immense.

If you use this workflow you should be able to create and render these scenes from scratch within 30 minutes.

LIGHTING

The lighting for this scene is similar to the other scenes in this book in terms of workflow. We are going to use the V-Ray Dome Light again and load it with a HDRI map.

The main emphasis is on saving time. We can have an incredibly fast turnaround with scenes like this if we are strategic in the way we set them up.

There are other methods such as using V-Ray lights to artificially illuminate the scene. For me this takes too long to set up and takes too long to render. The best designers are fast on their feet and using long-winded rendering methods is just not practical.

Open the exercise file named **06_Furniture_Mockup_ Start.max** from the project directory.

In this scene are two beautiful B&B Italia chairs with a table from Tom Dixon and a stunning lamp from Moooi. There are only 75,775 polygons in the scene so it will render pretty fast.

Now let's go ahead and set up V-Ray to begin with so that we can create the main light source.

In your Renderer dialog box, F10, set V-Ray as your production render engine (6.3).

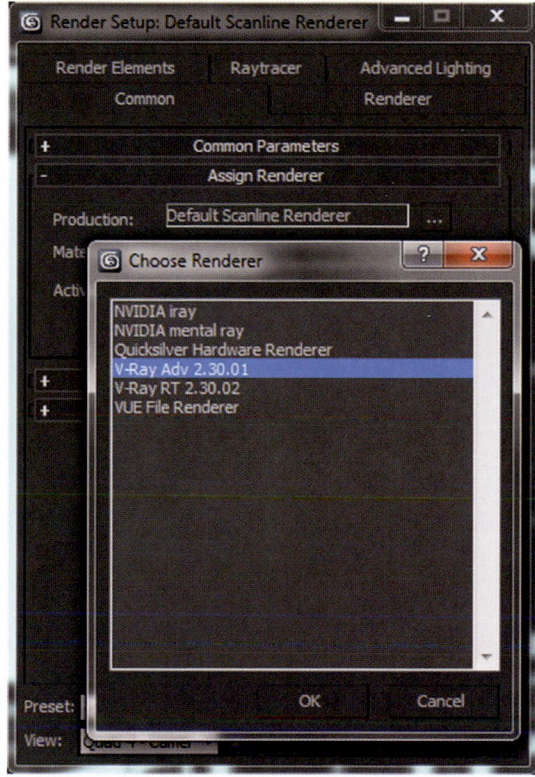

(6.3)

(6.4)

We now need to create the main V-Ray light that will cast our HDRI image onto our simple scene's geometry.

In the Create panel on the right-hand side of your screen select the light icon (6.4).

From the drop down menu choose V-Ray. In the object type select VRayLight.

In your top viewport click to place the light. I do try to place it in front of where my camera will be pointing so that I can easily select it when needed.

Now we need to adjust the light properties.

With the light still selected click on Modify in the panel to the right.

In the Parameters section, set the type to Dome in the drop down menu.

In the Intensity modifier make sure that the multiplier is set to 1.0.

Scroll down to the Options area. In here make sure that your settings reflect those shown (see over) (6.5).

In the Sampling settings set the Subdivs to 50.

Next in the Texture options enable Use texture. Set the Resolution to 2048.

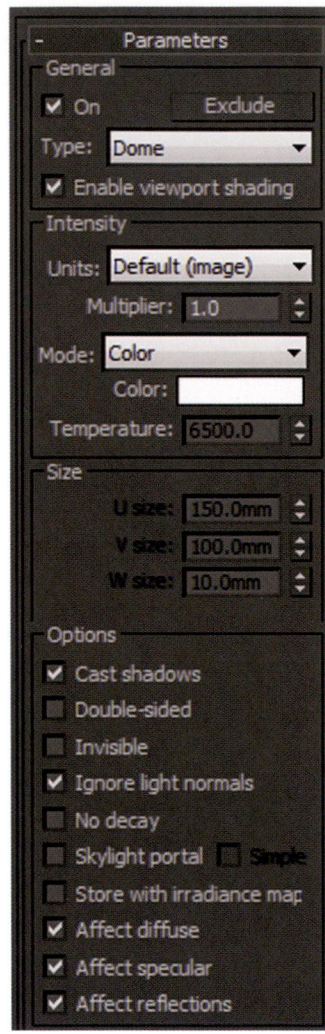

(6.5)

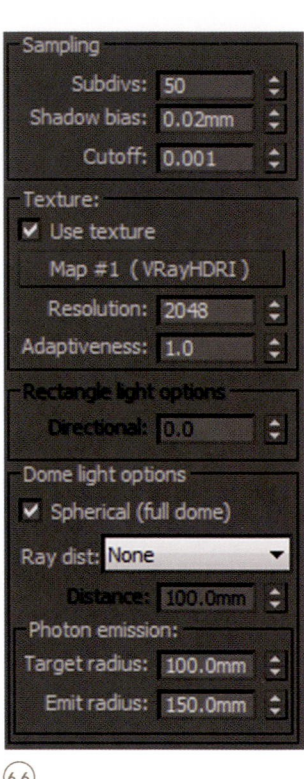

(6.6)

(6.7)

Just below you will see Dome light options, check the Spherical (full dome) option is enabled (6.6).

We need to now load the HDRI lighting file into our Materials Editor and then drag and drop the HDRI into the V-Ray light's distribution slot.

Press M on your keyboard to bring up your materials Editor.

Pick an empty material slot and rename it to HDRI. Now import a VRayHDRI map (6.7).

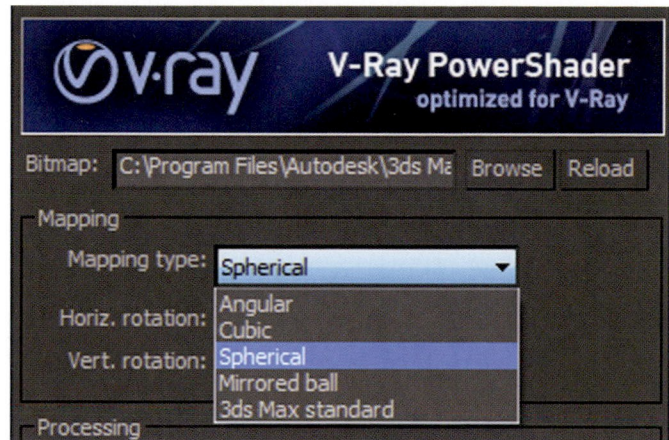

(6.8)

(6.9)

Make sure that the Mapping type is set to Spherical (6.8).

Next, select the V-Ray Dome Light and open up the modify tab. Scroll down to the Texture settings of the light and what you need to do now is to drag and drop the HDRI file from the Materials Editor into the empty slot with the name None (6.9).

When the Instance (Copy) Map box pops up, be sure to select the Instance method and press OK.

Because we are only using one HDRI file there is no need to add the HDRI to the background slot in the environment settings.

With this in mind make sure that the Invisible option in your V-Ray Dome Light is unchecked so that the textures in the scene will pick up the reflections of the light source (6.10).

That is it for this stage. This is a brief chapter so onwards and upwards we go and create the camera.

(6.10)

CAMERAS

Maintaining the theme of swiftness in this chapter we will keep the camera work fairly simple. One of the main benefits of working with a scene like this is that it acts as a platform for you to really experiment and develop your own camera and lighting styles.

The more you experiment with custom HDRI files combined with physically accurate camera settings the faster and more efficient you will become in creating any type of scenes for your clients in future.

This is the type of scene where you can really maximize on using added camera features such as depth of field given the shorter render times.

Continuing with our scene let's create a primary VRay Physical Camera from the Create panel .

Place the camera anywhere in your scene. I have taken the usual eye-level height of around 1500 mm in the Z direction.

In the camera's settings enter the following values as a rough starting point.

Let's input a fairly low value in the f-number option. Enter a value of 3.5.

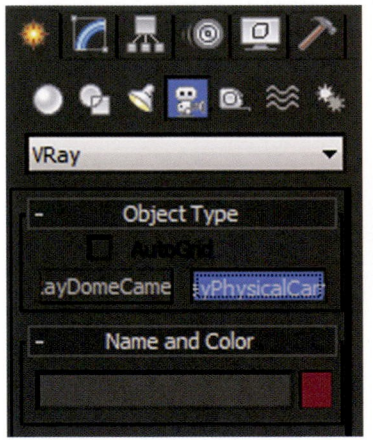

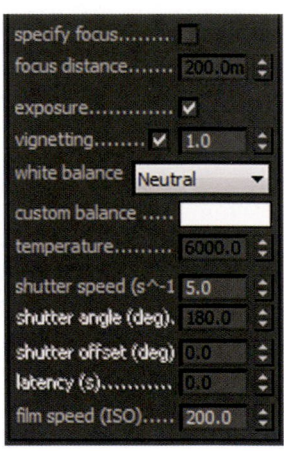

6.11

6.12

Just below you will find the Guess vert. button; click this while in your camera view to align your verticals.

We can select a Neutral white balance for now.

Set the shutter speed to 5.0 and the film speed (ISO) to 200.0. Here is what you should have 6.12.

Now we have the initial camera set up, let's adjust the V-Ray Render settings so we can create some output renders.

V-RAY SETTINGS

As you can see this scene is not a large one in terms of space occupation. This means that we can tailor the render settings to calculate the mock up without having to process information elsewhere.

Again the workflow is very simple in terms of activation of the main V-Ray Render elements.

For this scene I want to make sure that the detail is emphasized as much as possible.

The light calculation method needs to be precise and return realistic results. Here is how we will achieve this.

I am assuming that you are continuing with the previous file from where you set up the camera. If not you should be opening the file from the last point of saving.

Press F10 to open your Render settings dialog box.

V-Ray is already enabled so we can go ahead and key in the main settings.

At the top of the page next to Common, click the V-Ray tab .

In the V-Ray:: Frame buffer rollout make sure that Enable built-in Frame Buffer is enabled. Make sure that Get resolution from MAX is also enabled 6.14.

6.13

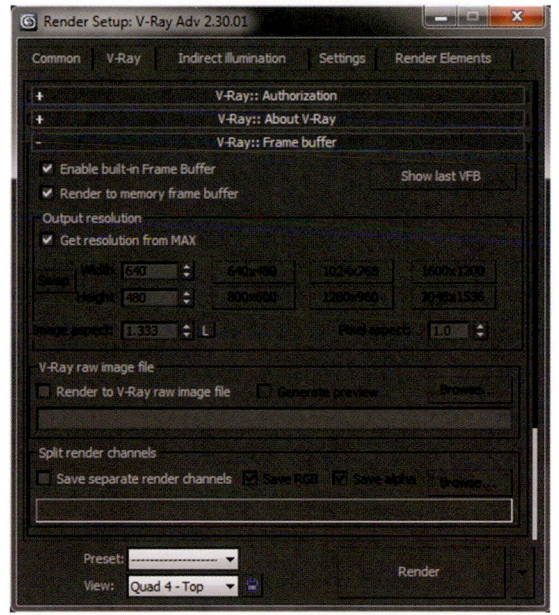

6.14

(6.15)

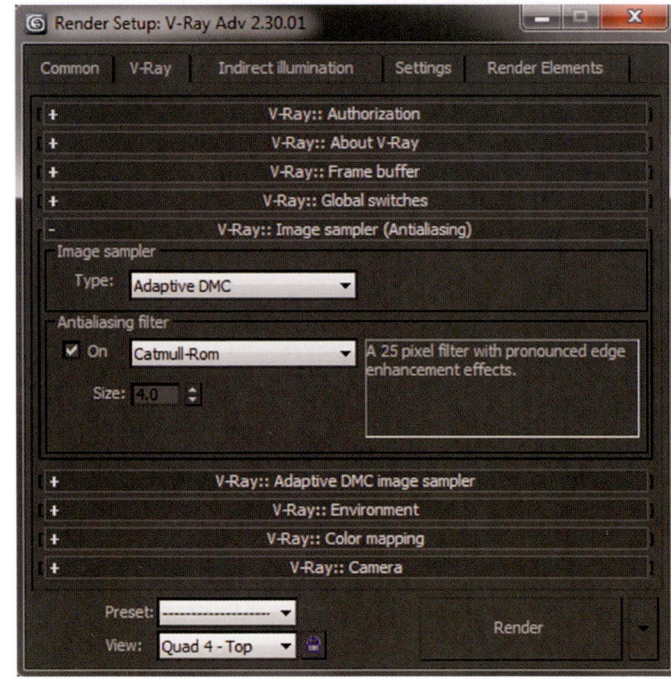

(6.16)

The next rollout we require is V-Ray:: Global switches. In the Lighting section, make sure that Hidden lights is checked and from the drop down menu Default lights are set to Off (6.15).

Just underneath you will find V-Ray Image sampler. In the Type section, select Adaptive DMC from the dropdown menu. Turn On the antialiasing filter and select Catmull Rom from the drop down menu (6.16).

Head down to the V-Ray:: Color mapping rollout. In the Type dropdown menu select Reinhard. Set the Burn value to 0.30 and make sure that the Sub-pixel mapping and the Clamp output options are enabled (6.17).

Back at the top of the Render scene dialog box click the Indirect Illumination tab (6.18).

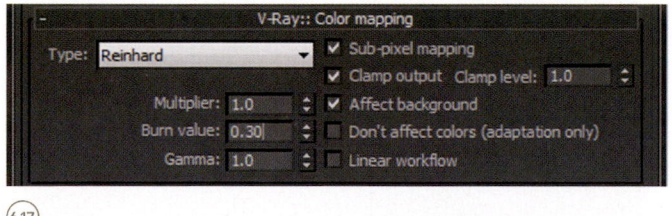

6.17

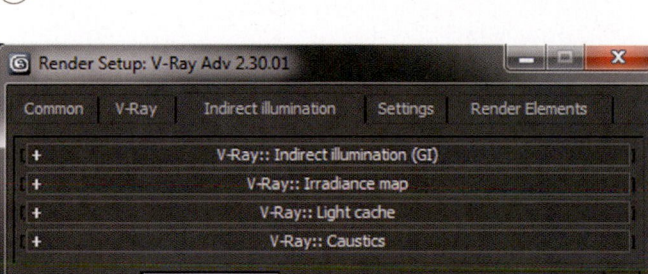

6.18

6.19

In the very first rollout named V-Ray:: Indirect illumination (GI), make sure that the On option is checked.

In the Primary bounces selection area choose Irradiance map.

Now in the Secondary bounces area choose Light cache from the drop down menu. While it seems that we are using these two methods a lot I do explain the other methods on the companion website.

For more information on this topic, please visit
WWW.FOCALPRESS.COM/CW/WYLDE!

Usually I use the other settings in here for animation purposes 6.19.

In the V-Ray:: Irradiance map rollout in the Built-in presets choose Medium from the drop down menu. Chaos Group did a fantastic job in creating presets that are built into V-Ray. The facility makes working with V-Ray a lot simpler for designers 6.20.

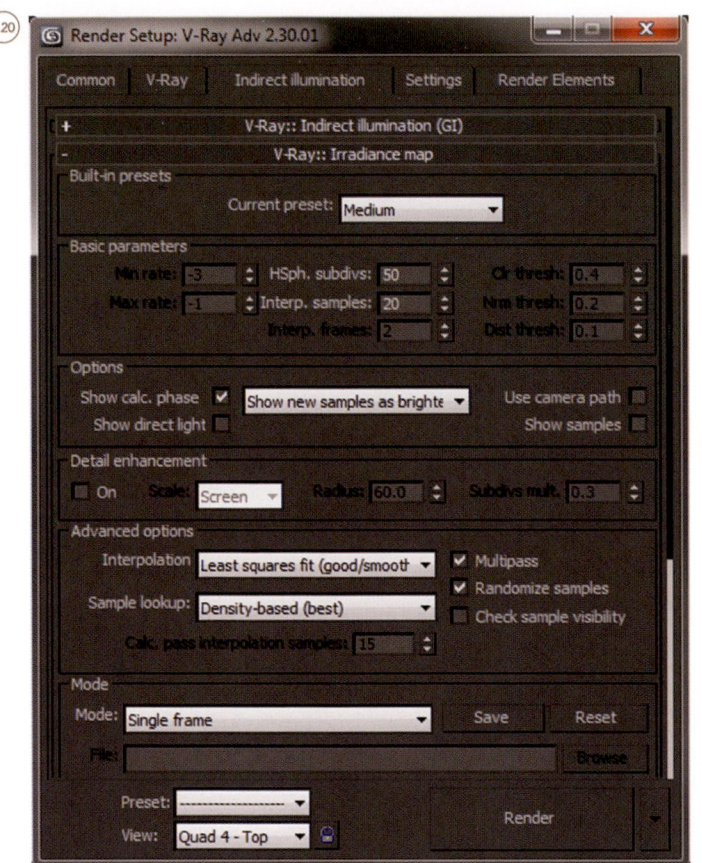

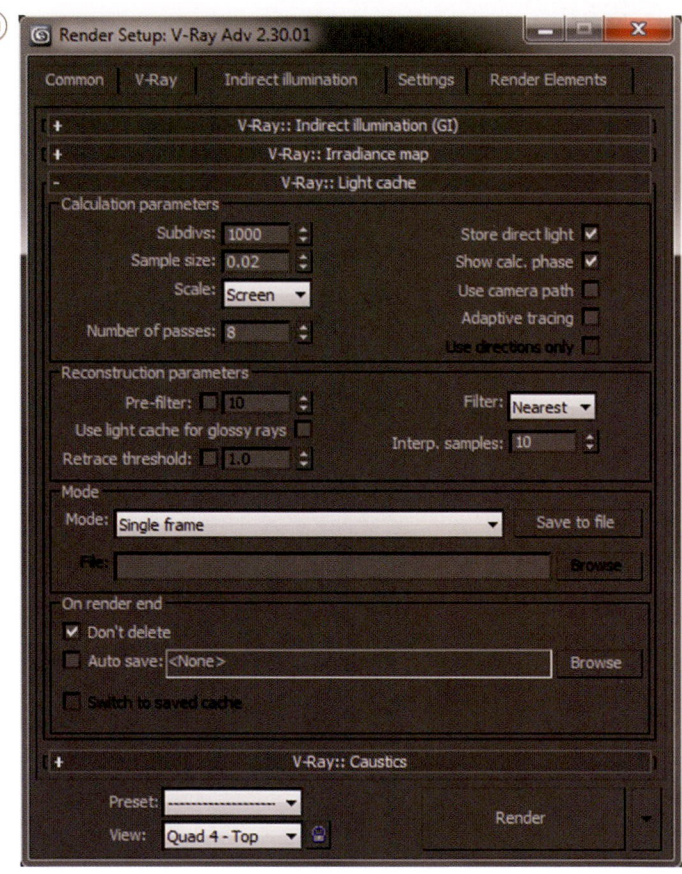

In the Options area to the right, make sure that Show calc. phase is enabled.

In the V-Ray:: Light cache rollout enter a value of 1000 in the Subdivs area. Finally make sure that the Show calc. phase is enabled (6.21).

This is pretty much it for now. The main aim of this section is to emphasize quality and speed. With that in mind let's go and render this scene.

RENDERING

Now you have the final elements of the scene all set up, you can now proceed and produce a test render by pressing F9 on your keyboard. The result should look like this 6.22.

The scene has a nice tone, provides us with realistic depth and is all in all rather well balanced. The image could benefit from a small amount of post-production work such as minor color and contrast filters.

6.22

Having said that, the image is good enough to be used straight from 3D Studio Max.

We can also go one step further in this scene by adding depth of field to the camera. Due to the space being relatively small, depth of field requires sufficient focal depth in order to achieve realistic results.

If you right-click your mouse button anywhere in the scene you will be presented with a pop up menu, in here select Unhide All (6.23).

Press C on your keyboard to choose which camera to render. Choose the DOF camera.

This particular camera has been set up to show you the alternative life style shots you can produce in this scene. If you render the DOF camera you will see that the floor lamp is out of focus and the primary focus is on the pictures on the wall. Of course rendering with DOF does take longer to complete compared to a camera without the function enabled (6.24).

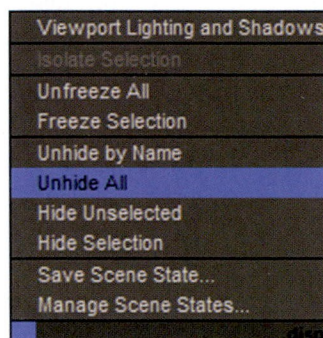

(6.23)

(6.24)

CHAPTER 7

EXTERIOR DAYTIME SCENES

DESIGN PROCESS

Having an architectural background certainly helps me focus when creating architectural exterior scenes.

My usual workflow would be to start by obtaining the architect's design scheme, depending on what stage the design is at. If you have designed the scheme, then that is a bonus as you will have a clear vision of what look and feel you require.

A fundamental understanding of how light works is essential if you want to achieve realistic results. Light is everywhere, sounds simple enough, but light also bounces. This has an effect on how a surface or material performs when hit by direct light or indeed artificial light. Light also affects the way that colored surfaces and materials bounce color around a scene. What is truly nice about exterior scenes is the mix of rugged materials with slick, polished, almost conformative materials. Understanding how light works will enable you to seamlessly mix the two.

The proper use of materials is essential if you are seeking to achieve a realistic result. Created materials such as aluminum, glass, wood, grass, soil, chrome and related industrial materials require the correct properties in order to function realistically.

For this particular exercise I have created a mockup of a contemporary residential scheme that consists of a rather simple concrete structure together with large open glazed areas. There is a peripheral timber cladding element that acts as an exoskeleton fusing the house together and connects it with its surroundings.

The selection of the background lighting source is incredibly important in a daytime scene. It must be high quality, sharp and relevant to your scene.

If I use a low dynamic range HDRI then the shadows will be simply awful, the materials will look cheap and patchy and this is certainly not what the client will be expecting.

Collecting the resources for architectural scenes is incredibly important. Wherever I can create my own textures and model my own elements I do. There are times when you will need to rely on other resources that are available commercially.

One of the main elements for any designer, architect or enthusiast to strategize when creating exterior renders is location, location, location.

It is one task to model a piece of architecture, it is quite another to create accurate landscaping that does not highlight or bring into question the authenticity of your render. Couple this with the fact that trees take forever to render, you are stuck with a balance of time versus quality versus getting paid!

Luckily there are resources online to ease the burden. Items such as foliage, trees, vehicles and other models exist in the form of purchasable libraries. I have listed many of these on the companion website.

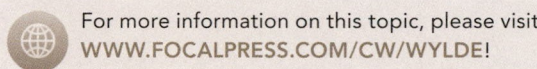

For more information on this topic, please visit
WWW.FOCALPRESS.COM/CW/WYLDE!

Another concept is to photo match your building into a photograph. Using camera tracking methods can be tricky, but if mastered can be a very effective medium. On the other hand I know that often designers do not have the time for luxuries and as such I will show you my practical way.

The method that we will be undertaking is a sort of blend between a photomontage and traditional visualization methods. HDRI lends itself particularly well to scenes that require a seamless integration of subject matter and a photographic environment.

Scene props and peripherals are essential. If you are creating a scene for a contemporary piece of architecture with large glazed areas, then you will achieve an even better result if you place furniture in the interior space.

Glass is opaque; if you can make the spaces look occupied, then you have won half of the battle convincing someone that the image is real.

The same can be said for garden furniture. With the careful placement of external furniture combined with depth of field, truly realistic results can be achieved.

SketchUp is an essential tool for exterior scenes. Simplified modeling techniques enable you to think about detail without being overwhelmed with the sheer amount of work that needs to be done.

Architectural visualization for exterior scenes is really about selling a product, someone's dream; you should have fun doing it, you should strive to be different and you should certainly read the remainder of this chapter if you want to boost your skills!

Let's crack on and tackle the exercise.

LIGHTING

Are we aiming to imbue sadness or happiness? I ask this because another of my pet hates is seeing architectural renders spoilt by what can only be described as miserable lighting. One would assume that the very notion of creating something that resembles another's dream means that it should be in fact happily portrayed.

Deciding on your lighting methods upfront before you even begin to render, apply materials and fiddle with cameras, is essential. We want beautifully brightly lit scenes with the correct physically balanced lighting.

The geography of the site in question plays a crucial part in the fabric of the scene. If for example the site is on a level plane and has no foliage surrounding it, then you are going to be stuck for additional realistic elements such as reflections in your glass. I always find it useful to take a look at Google Earth, see what surrounds your site. If your project is theoretical then choose a site, factor in some real-world scenarios; this will not only give your project additional depth, but it will also aid the development of your research skills as well as your analytical skills.

Making positive use of HDRI files stops us from trying to guess nature's way. We are in fact on nature's side, using geographic referenced atmospheric lighting in a way that requires little guesswork.

Understandably you are going to find it difficult if you want to mimic the lighting in Turkey and you live in Kansas City, you cannot go and shoot a custom HDRI file for your project or coursework.

Professionals with wonderful budgets on the other hand may have the chance to visit a site that they have been contracted to design. It would be incredibly beneficial to take their cameras and shoot an onsite HDRI.

What time of day are we rendering? Why is this even important? As the sun rises on a clear day it casts beautiful fuzzy shadows complemented with warm sunlight onto objects. On the other hand the sun can barely cast directional shadows at 16:00 p.m. while it is raining in London. So we have to make a decision so that we can match the direct sunlight to the HDRI file to cast accurate shadows.

All of the above needs to be pondered before you begin to even open 3D Studio Max.

For this scene we are going to use the HDRI method of lighting of course and utilize the V-Ray sunlight source.

Now navigate yourself to the project folders and open the **07_Exterior_Day_Start.max** file.

In this file you will find a simple, fully textured scene with peripheral items such as trees, foliage, garden furniture and vehicles contained within.

Sometimes when using trees in your scene you can experience slow graphic user interface feedback, or slow regenerating viewports.

To counter this I adjust the properties of the tree so that I only see boxes instead of the final mesh. Do not worry, the trees still render, just make sure that your landscaping layout is pretty much fixed otherwise you'll be switching back and forth between viewing options. Alternatively you can utilize the import overlay method of merging files. I do the same for items such as vehicles and furniture if I know they are in fixed positions.

In the top viewport, T on your keyboard, go ahead and create a V-Ray Dome Light. This can be found on the right-hand side of your screen under the lighting creation panel (7.1).

Place the lighting anywhere in the scene, preferably so that it is easy to select in your future camera view.

In the Parameters section under General, switch the Type to Dome from the drop down list (7.2).

In doing this we are instructing the light to act differently in terms of its distribution.

(7.1)

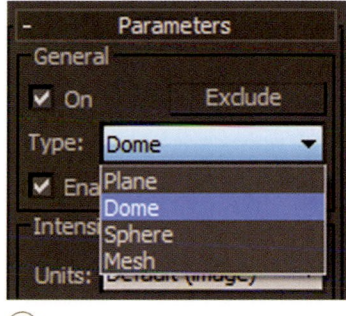
(7.2)

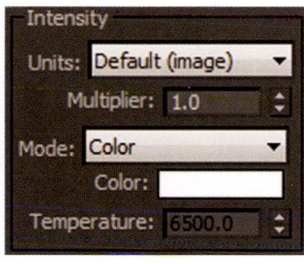
(7.3)

Further down you should see the Intensity section. In here keep the Units as Default (image). Also keep the Multiplier set to a value of 1.0 (7.3).

Scroll down to the Options section. In here are all the attributes that dictate the behavior of the light. We want the light to cast shadows so enable Cast shadows. Leave Double-sided unchecked.

Make sure that the Invisible box is enabled. I will explain this later when we import our light source HDRI file.

Here is an overview of what should and should not be checked (7.4).

Navigate your way down to the next bunch of settings called Sampling. This is incredibly important. I receive a lot of inquiries through my website asking why people's scenes look so patchy when rendering with HDRI files. The usual suspect is that the light source subdivisions are not set high enough.

Alternatively it can be a combination of the Subdivs and Resolution value of the source HDRI in the Texture settings. Some people leave these settings low to try and achieve a lower render time. I would strongly advise people not to do this.

In the Texture options enable the Use texture function. With this selected we are instructing the light to not emit just a color but to emit a texture. In this case it will be our HDRI file. Insert a value of 24 in the Subdivs section. This value can go up to a limit of 1000. I suggest not going more than 100. It can affect the render time.

Set the Resolution to 2048, which is the highest value you can go to. Some people may say this is insane, it will take forever to render. Well, those people may only be using one HDRI file in their scene which is 200 MB. In this case I would agree and lower the value, but we are actually

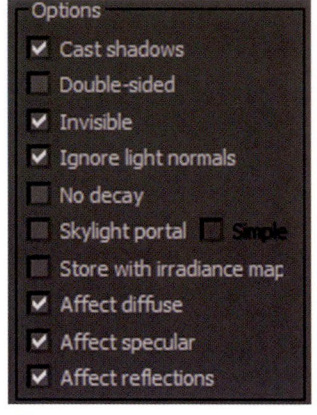

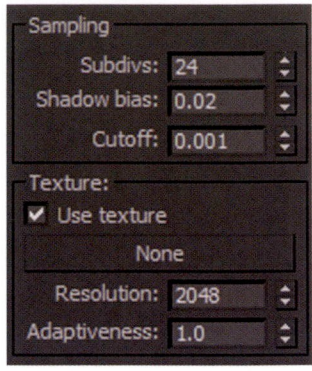

7.4 7.5

using two HDRI files. We will return to this later on in this chapter. For now make sure that your settings resemble this (7.5).

Just underneath the Texture options is another small group of settings labeled Dome Light options. This is often overlooked and makes a world of difference if enabled.

If this is not enabled when we come to render we will see a large horizontal line below which all will all appear black. More importantly we will have zero light emission from below the horizon line. Enabling this means we are able to use the whole HDRI lighting file instead of 50 percent. Opposite is an example of not utilizing this option (7.6).

So make sure that the Spherical (full dome) is enabled.

(7.6)

Open your Materials browser by pressing M on your keyboard. If your Materials Editor appears as the annoying new Slate mode, and in fact you are rather partial to being old school, then you can change back to the standard stacked Materials Editor by going to the menu at the top and navigating to Rendering, then choosing Materials Editor and choosing Compact Materials Editor.

(7.7)

(7.8)

Now we need to import our HDRI files into the Materials Editor. Choose a blank material and select the Get Material icon (7.7).

The Materials/Map Browser should pop up. Within here scroll down to the Maps section and select the Standard from the subsection. Scroll down to the VRayHDRI slot and double click it. It will load a small black box into your Materials Editor slot (7.8).

In the Materials Editor you will see that a V-Ray Power Shader has loaded. This shader is wonderful; it enables us to alter the HDRI files from one location.

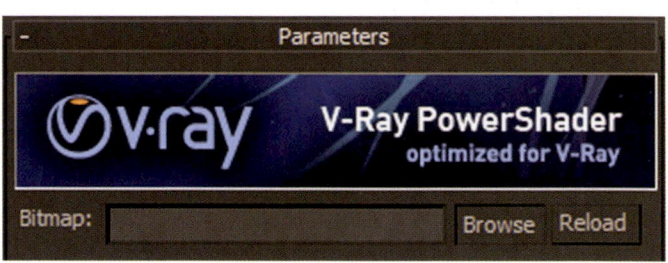

(7.9)

Where it says bitmap: click the Browse button and go to the 07_Exterior_Daytime project folder and within here select the maps folder (7.9).

In the maps folder is an HDRI folder. Contained within this folder are two HDRI files. I mentioned above that some people use only one HDRI file and apply it to their scene. We will be using two for two reasons.

First, one HDRI is for the outdoor background which will be rendered in the final scene, so in this case the quality of the image needs to be rather high, otherwise there will be a large contrasting quality issue between our rendered geometry and the background image. The quality of reflections in objects can be seen also, so we need to make sure that the reflections are accurate and proportional to the scene's scale.

Second, using this high-quality HDRI file as the light emitter will significantly increase the render time. So instead we will use a slightly blurred version of the file. This also gives us incredibly soft shadows which will add an increasing level of realism to the scene.

Once the HDRI has been loaded, you will see a small preview in your Materials Editor. It will also look distorted. Don't panic, we will be dictating the mapping method.

In the Mapping options select the drop down menu which will say Angular. Choose Spherical from the list. Now your preview looks better. Leave everything else as is (7.10).

Let's now instruct our V-Ray Dome Light to emit our HDRI file. Select the light and navigate to the light's properties. In here scroll down to the Texture options section (7.11).

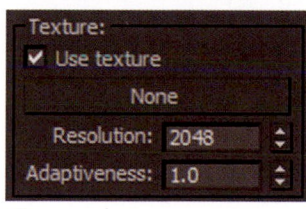

Very simply we are going to drag the HDRI material from the Materials Editor and drop it into the Texture slot within the Light's properties. Like this (7.12):

7.12

7.13

When the Instance (Copy) Map pop up appears you need to select Instance and press OK. This is important because any changes you make to the HDRI will automatically be updated rather than having to drag and drop the HDRI into the light's properties again 7.13.

Almost there, stick with me! Now we need to load the large HDRI file into our scene to act as the background image.

As before, select a blank material and import the large HDRI file from the same location. Make sure the Mapping Type is set to Spherical.

A final important part is telling Max to use this high-quality HDRI as the visible backdrop. Press 8 on your keyboard to open the Environment and Effects dialog.

Under the Common Parameters Section you will see Background. Check the Use Map to enable the texture rollout slot. Simply drag and drop the high-quality HDRI file from the Materials Editor to the empty slot in the Environment Map slot. Here is the backdrop HDR file we are using 7.14.

When the Instance (Copy) Map pop up appears, be sure to select Instance.

We now need to create a light source to act as the sun. This light will create beautiful soft shadows and cast warm light onto our geometry.

In the Create panel, go to the Light section and choose VRay from the drop down menu.

Let's go ahead and create a V-Ray Sun. In your top viewport choose a location in the bottom right-hand corner of your viewport and drag the target to the center of the house 7.15.

7.14

In the Modify panel on the right we will now change the properties of the sun so that the lighting levels are correct and balanced.

Under the VRaySun Parameters, drop the Intensity multiplier to 0.01. This does seem low; however if you do a test render later on with the multiplier set to 0.5 then you will see why.

You can also change the Shadow subdivs to a value of 5.

Finally reposition the VRay Sun in the Z direction so that you are achieving a nice angle in order to cast shadows.

Remember lighting is just one part of this process; none of the above will even matter unless we can place cameras in the scene with the correct settings to give us the desired output.

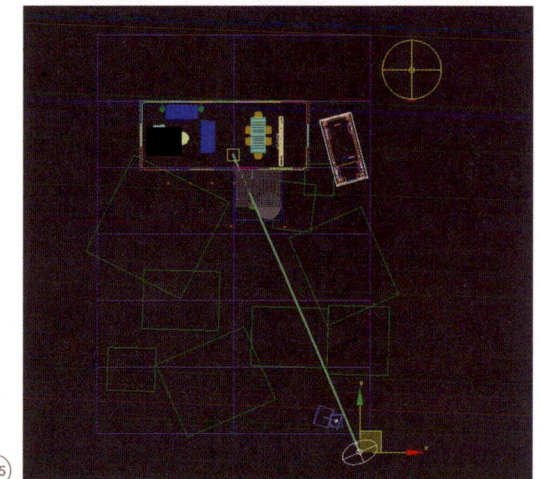

7.15

CAMERAS

To best accentuate architectural scenes I usually place my camera at eye level which is 1590 mm (I do suppose it depends on how tall you are!).

The other relevant choice you must make is what size of image you are rendering and how it correlates to the camer's aperture. For example if you are rendering in the preset size of HDTV 1920 × 1080, but have your camera set to 35 mm, then we will have render issues with the final render output in terms of composition.

In my opinion you should check www.archdaily.com for the best examples of architectural and interior photography.

The V-Ray Physical Camera settings for daytime scenes are critical. Again we must be process-orientated and match our camera settings to the HDRI file as much as possible.

There are also other factors that can increase the realism of architectural exterior scenes such as depth of field. Enabling this feature will increase the render time significantly; however it does produce phenomenal results.

When it comes to creating cameras for external scenes, there are literally hundreds of combinations to achieve a well-balanced image. When people think of outdoor photography they think sunny day with a bright blue sky. That's great if you live in San Francisco, but not everyone does. If you live in the UK then you will be sitting around for a long time waiting for a sunny day. So we have to adapt and configure the camera settings to deal with a whole range of environments.

This is particularly poignant in the case of creating 3D visualizations. You may have a client who requires a rainy day scene, or overcast scene, so you have to be prepared. Luckily for this scene we are using a nice bright sky so we will adapt the camera settings to best suit the environment.

Create a V-Ray Physical Camera from the Creation panel on the right-hand side of your screen 7.16 .

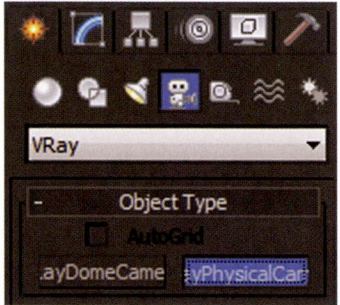

(7.17)

Place the camera in your scene where you deem fit. Try to capture foreground details that can be emphasized while maintaining focus on the main structure.

With the camera selected make the Z value 1590 to place it at eye level. Do the same for the camera pointer.

When photographing sunny scenes there is what's known as the sunny 16 rule where you should keep the f-number set to 16, keep the ISO value as low as possible and simply adjust the shutter speed to suit.

So with this in mind let's put the theory into a virtual reality (7.17).

As this is a daytime scene the camera values will obviously differ from the interior scenes in the previous chapters.

The process of refining the setting is the same however. Manual photography during the day can be tedious. There are a lot of factors to bear in mind, and unfortunately we cannot use an auto function here. Ultimately a little tenacity on your part is needed.

As with the interior scene earlier in this book, we have to adjust a significant portion of the camera's settings to achieve a realistic result.

With the camera selected bring up the camera's properties in the Modify section on the right.

In the Basic parameters section adjust the f-number to 16.0.

Don't forget to click the Guess vert. button to align your verticals.

Set the White balance to Neutral.

Just beneath you will see the shutter speed (s^-1), set the value to 0.05.

Finally adjust the film speed ISO to a value of 100.0.

Setting up our cameras for external scenes with the workflow we are using enables you to place a camera anywhere and render with the same look and feel, so go ahead and place as many cameras as you like and experiment with the scene.

Now we are ready to finalize the render settings.

V-RAY SETTINGS

Since exterior scenes have a significant amount of light bouncing around, we need to make sure that the method of rendering complements and highlights the main details in surface textures etc.

To achieve this we will make a modification to the V-Ray render settings. At this point you may be thinking that the settings are virtually the same for all scenes. Well, this is far from the truth. As I am showing you my way of creating scenes, these are the settings that best perform for me and my requirements in order to successfully deliver a quality product to my clients.

While interior scenes may share similar settings with the mockup scenes for example, exterior scenes require refinements through specific data entry.

We will be effectively following the previous methods of rendering that have utilized the Irradiance map and Light cache for the Global illumination calculations.

Changing the Global illumination calculation methods will affect the overall render time so be warned when you are experimenting.

With the project exercise still open go ahead and press F10 on your keyboard to bring up the Render setup window.

(7.18)

V-Ray is already enabled as the production renderer.

From the tabs at the top click on the V-Ray tab (7.18).

From the V-Ray:: Frame buffer rollout enable the built-in Frame Buffer. Make sure the Get resolution from MAX is enabled (7.19).

Next open the V-Ray:: Global Switches rollout. In here uncheck Hidden lights. Select Off from the Default lights drop down menu (7.20).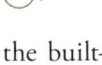

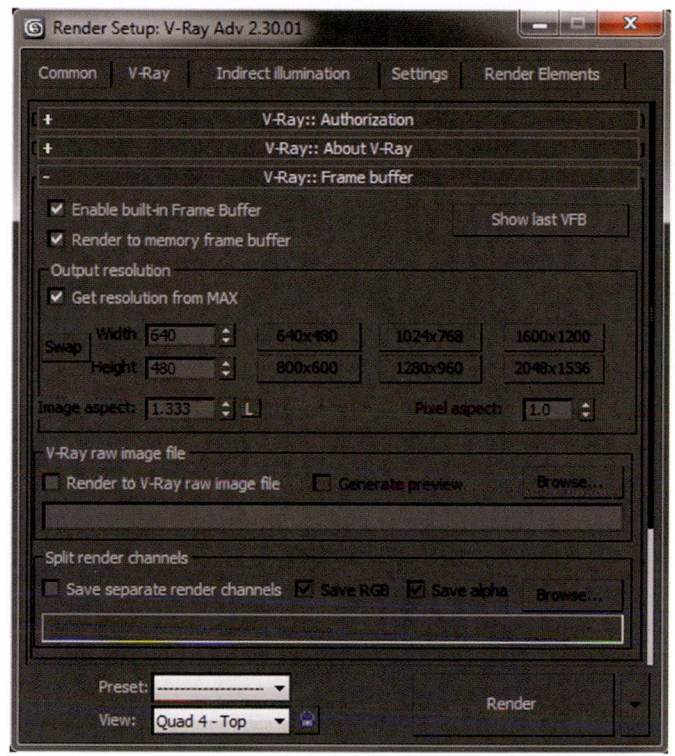

7.19

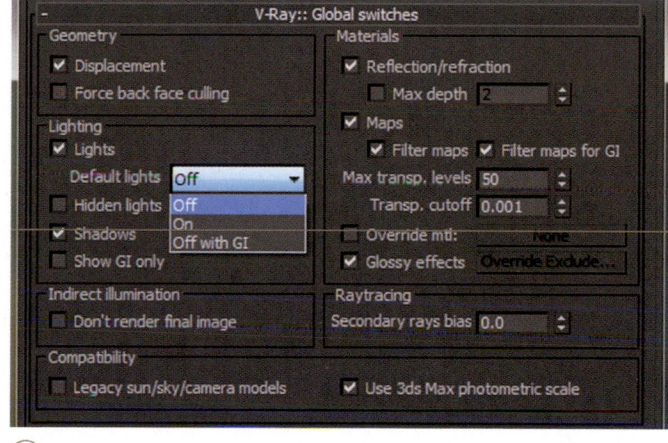

7.20

You should find the V-Ray:: Image sampler (Antialiasing) rollout just below the Global switches rollout.

In here change the Image sampler to Adaptive DMC from the drop down menu.

For this scene I want my rendered geometry to seem sharp and accentuated, so I want an emphasized filter. To do this we will be using the Catmull-Rom Antialiasing Filter. You can choose this from the drop down menu (see over) 7.21.

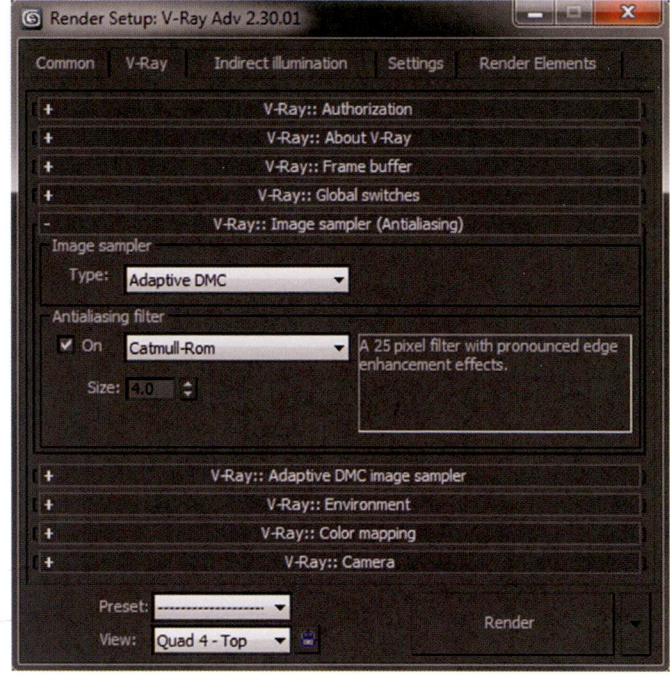

Scroll down to the V-Ray:: Color mapping rollout. Now because we are using a particularly large HDRI file containing so many temperature depths, combined with a VRay Sun, we need to make sure that the scene is not returned overbright and remains realistically balanced.

In the Type selection area choose Reinhard from the drop down menu. The reason why I use Reinhard a lot is because it is a mixture of two color mapping types. It is a dynamic mix between exponential color mapping and linear color mapping. Why is this so important? Well, if we use another singular method of color mapping we will not be able to achieve realistic toning using the method of HDRI lighting.

Reinhard is easy to control from a value of 0.0 to 1.0 meaning that the closer to the value 1.0 the more burnt out the final render will be. I cover each of the settings and what they do on the companion website. For now go ahead and adjust the Burn value to 0.12 (7.22).

For more information on this topic, please visit
WWW.FOCALPRESS.COM/CW/WYLDE!

Back to the top of the F10 Render setup dialog box, open up the Indirect Illumination tab (7.23).

In the V-Ray:: Indirect illumination rollout make sure that the On is enabled.

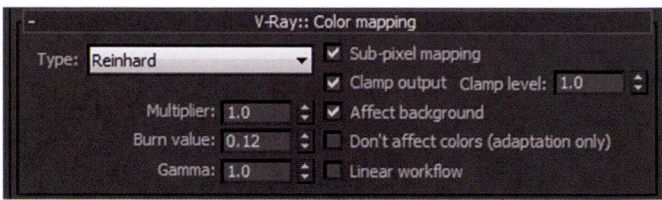

7.22

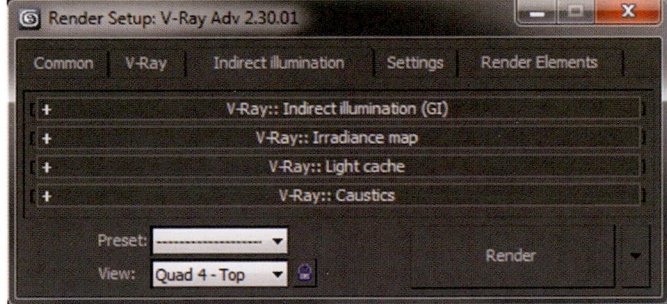

(7.23)

In the Primary bounces section set the GI engine to Irradiance map. Now set the Secondary bounces GI engine to Light cache (7.24).

In the V-Ray:: Irradiance map rollout there is a section named Built-in presets. From the drop down menu choose Medium. In the options area just below make sure that Show calc. phase is enabled (7.25).

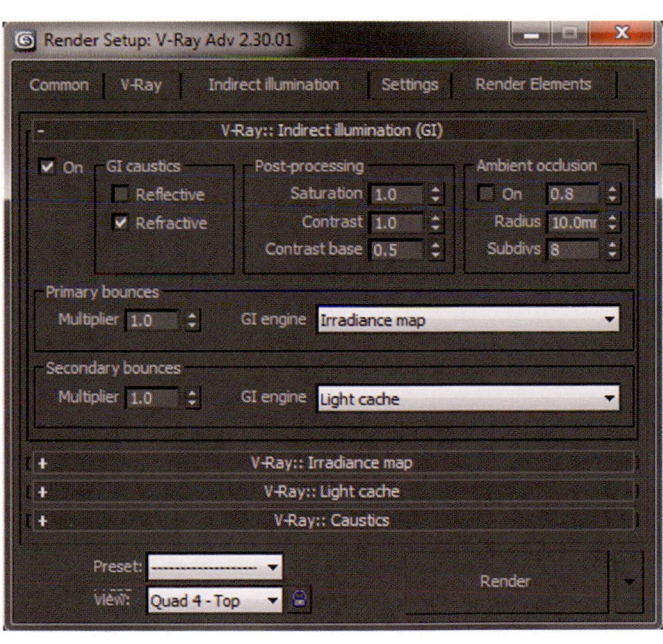

(7.24)

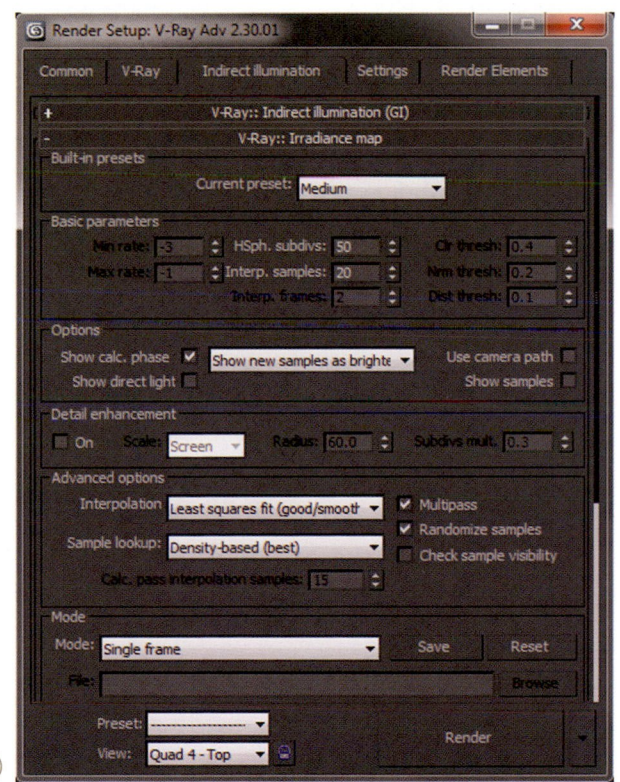

(7.25)

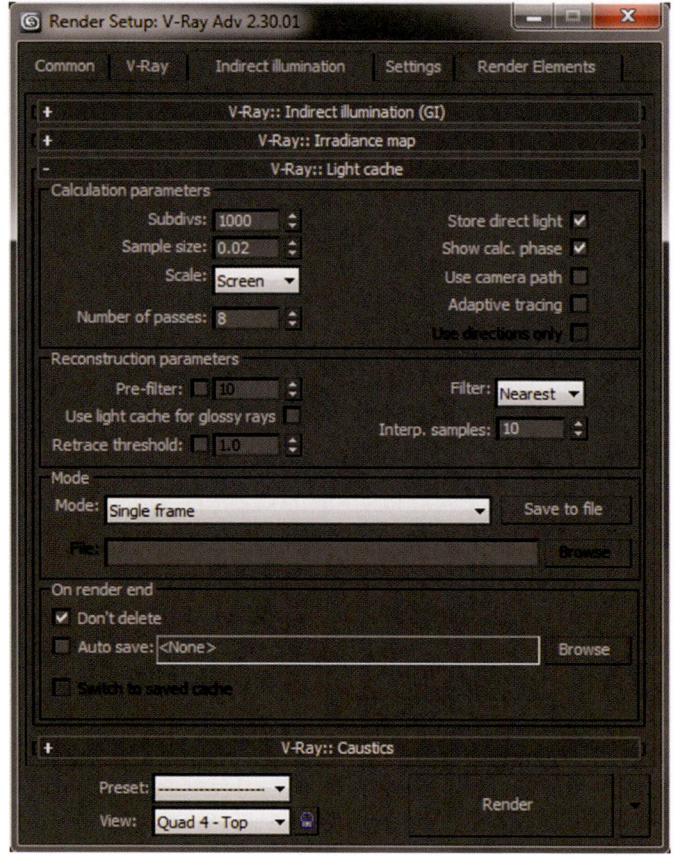

Just underneath open the V-Ray:: Irradiance map rollout. In here we need to input sufficient settings in order to render a quality scene. As a general rule, keeping in mind we need to stick to fast render times, in the calculation parameters I set the Subdivs to equal 50 percent of my output render size. So for example the width of the render we will produce is 1920. Fifty percent of this is 960, so we can enter a value of 960–1000. In this case you can input 1000. Keep the sample size set to 0.02.

We want to instantly see the results as the render screen builds so enable Show calc. phase on the right (7.26).

Now we have the majority of the base settings set up.

You can now start rendering your scene to see what kind of finish you are presented with. Like everything in design, when you are replicating reality in a digital format there are always tweaks to be made.

RENDERING

Press F9 to create a test render. This should take 40 minutes or so. Your scene should produce an image that resembles the following, depending on your chosen camera position of course (7.27).

I am relatively happy with the output for this scene. I do believe however that we can achieve a richer image by adjusting the camera settings. Go ahead and change your camera settings. Keep the f-number set to 16.0. Change the shutter

(7.27)

(7.28)

speed to a value of 0.24. Finally change the film speed ISO to a value of 200.0 .Now press F9 and render the scene again (7.28) .

This is much better, the shadows are deeper and the overall color and depth of the scene are well balanced. As with everything in design, it is opinion that counts, so if you have the time try alternate camera settings, render them, print them out and pin them up. Involve the team so that you can unify a decision for finals.

Again adding additional elements to the scene increases the render time. Try and keep your foliage numbers down as well as trees and vehicles.

If you do have the requirement for copious amounts of trees to be placed in your scene then I highly suggest using V-Ray proxies. These proxies are essential for scenes that sometimes 3D Studio Max cannot cope with when rendering. These are external files loaded into 3D Studio Max at render time. They do not take up any resources in your scene while you are modeling so you can freely move around.

Whenever I try to convince someone that HDRI lighting is an essential skill that they should discover and explore, the usual response I get is negative, solely based on items like trees not being able to render in short amounts of time, or simply Max crashes when rendering.

These trees were rendered in 00:35:00 at HDTV 1920 × 1080 .

So if you are looking to work with smoother files and have less lag in your viewports then V-Ray proxies are the way to go. You will find out how to create and use these files effectively on this book's companion website.

> For more information on this topic, please visit
> WWW.FOCALPRESS.COM/CW/WYLDE!

If you want to take your scene further, try enabling the DOF function on the camera and experimenting with the position of the camera to achieve realistic results.

CHAPTER 8

EXTERIOR EVENING SCENES

DESIGN PROCESS

Truth be told, exterior evening scenes are my favorite. If you can master the balance between twilight and artificial light while emphasizing materials, then you have the potential to create striking renders.

In this chapter we cover the essential elements to be able to adequately set up evening exterior environments combined with complementing camera settings. It is a very straightforward workflow.

In order to successfully create detailed renders you must start from the beginning.

What do I mean by this?

Model in detail and try to not cut corners. There is nothing worse than a third party saying 'What about the drainpipes?'.

Utilizing all the information available regarding a specific design scheme including specifications and yet again reference imagery is pivotal.

I often come across images with such potential that are unfortunately ruined by poor attention to details—details such as repetitive textures visible on brick or concrete surfaces, glass that does not reflect properly, poor foreground textures etc. These critical elements can be planned upfront with the right workflow.

If you are modeling from architect's drawings then try and obtain the AutoCAD versions so that you can build the model in SketchUp in tremendous detail.

You should always model to a scale. I create all of my scenes in metric, specifically millimeters.

SketchUp lends itself very well to rescaling objects and full scenes even if you have started in inches and want to use the metric scale instead.

Use layers where possible. When you import the SketchUp into 3D Studio Max the same layer-naming conventions are used. This is the same for any instanced objects or groups. You need not export a 3ds from SketchUp. 3D Studio Max has a function to directly import Skp files.

I cannot emphasize enough how important it is to have detail in your scene. In this particular exercise you will see that the apartment has an external aluminum cladding system. The amount of times I have seen just a picture or texture of aluminum applied as a material to a plane surface is incredible. Instead try and model the sections of cladding with the correct nominal offsets etc. so that the depth is increased in the scene.

This also means that accurate performing V-Ray power shaders can be applied to the mesh without having to cheat with photographic textures.

In this exercise scene there is a vast amount of glazing. Contributing factors to the level of realism come from items modeled such as glazing channels, shadow gaps, interior loose elements and the choice of materials.

Again if you can obtain a drawing package that includes a lighting layout, then this is an additional bonus to your workflow. You can configure the lighting to calculate the lighting levels and achieve a physically balanced render. Adding the actual light fixture as a 3D model will also add to the overall depth and realism of the scene.

Most exterior scenes will show at least a glimpse of the interior space. Using this to your advantage rather than treating it as an element to cover up will certainly strengthen your visuals.

In this scene you will see plenty of furniture and artwork. There are subtle features such as the air conditioning linear slot diffusers in the ceiling that just balance the space out and increase the realism.

So with this in mind let's go ahead and open the scene and see what we have to play with.

Open the file **08_Exterior_Evening_Start.max** from the project exercise folder. Here is a preview of the scene (8.1).

(8.1)

LIGHTING

In this section we need to set up the main indoor artificial lighting and the evening environment light source.

The interior space once lit will create some very interesting results given that this is a dual aspect piece of architecture. Dual aspect means significant glazed areas on both sides of the building.

Let's proceed and set up the HDRI lighting first. As you will have noticed by now, the workflow in terms of setting up V-Ray environment lighting is starting to become second nature. You will soon be able to do this within minutes.

In the top viewport, T on your keyboard, go ahead and create a VRay Dome Light. This can be found on the right-hand side of your screen under the lighting creation panel .

Place the lighting anywhere in the scene, preferably so that it is easy to select in your future camera view.

In the Parameters section under General, switch the Type to Dome from the drop down list .

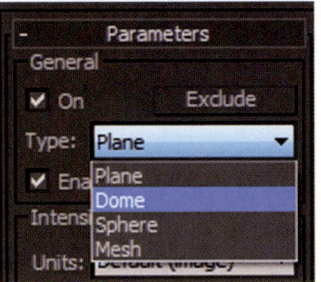
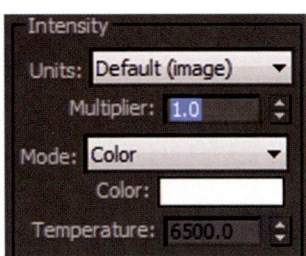

In doing this we are instructing the light to act differently in terms of its distribution method.

Just below you should see the Intensity section. Keep the Units set as Default (image). Also set the Multiplier to a value of 1.0 ⑻.⁴ .

Zip down to the Options section. In here collectively are the controllable attributes that dictate the behavior and performance of the light. We want the light to cast shadows so enable Cast shadows. Leave Double-sided unchecked.

Make sure that the Invisible checkbox is reading as active. Here is a preview of what should and should not be enabled (8.5).

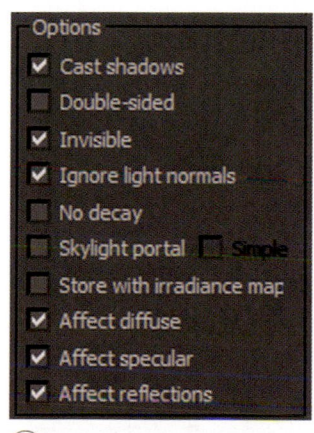

(8.5)

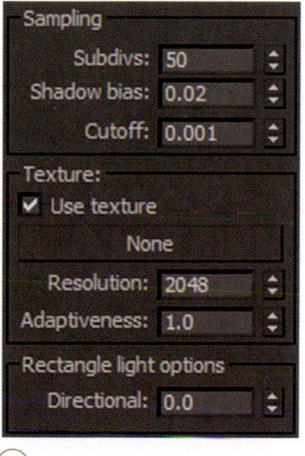

(8.6)

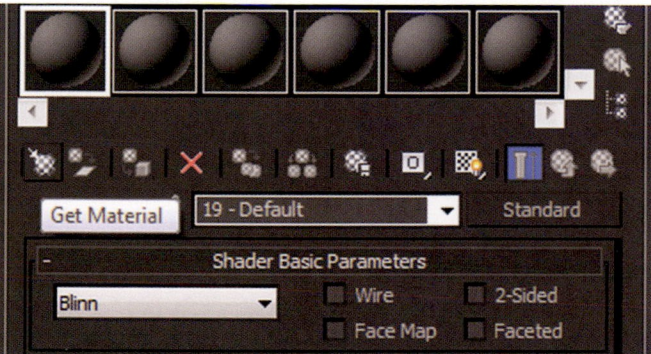

(8.7)

Navigate your way down to the next group of settings named Sampling.

In the Texture options enable the Use texture function. With this selected we are instructing the light to not emit just a color but also a texture.

In this case it will be our evening HDRI file. Insert a value of 50 in the Subdivs section.

Set the Resolution to 2048, which is the highest value you can input (8.6).

Make sure that the Spherical (full dome) is enabled.

Open your Materials browser by pressing M on your keyboard. We now need to import our HDRI files into the Materials Editor. Choose a blank material and select the Get Material icon (8.7).

The Materials/Map browser should pop up. Within here scroll down to the Maps section and select the Standard from the subsection. Scroll down to the VRayHDRI slot and double click it (8.8).

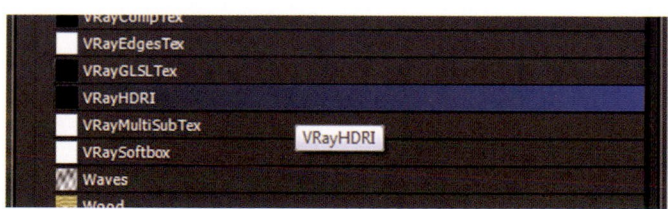

(8.8)

(8.9)

It will load a small black box into your Materials Editor slot (8.9).

In the Materials Editor you will see a V-Ray PowerShader has loaded. This shader is wonderful; it enables us to alter the HDRI files from one location.

Where it says Bitmap, click the Browse button and go to the 08_Exterior_Evening project folder and within here select the Maps folder.

In the Maps folder is a HDRI folder. Contained within this folder are two HDRI files. Go ahead and import the HDRI_EVE_LOW.hdr

Once the HDRI has been loaded, you will see a small preview in your Materials Editor. It will also look distorted. Don't panic, we will be dictating the mapping method.

In the Mapping options select the drop down menu which will say Angular. Choose Spherical from the list. Now your preview looks better. Leave everything else as is (8.10).

Let's now instruct our VRay Dome Light to emit our HDRI file. Select the light and navigate to the light's properties. In here scroll down to the Texture options section (8.11).

Very simply we are going to drag the HDRI material from the Materials Editor and drop it into the Texture slot within the light's properties (see opposite) (8.12):

(8.10)

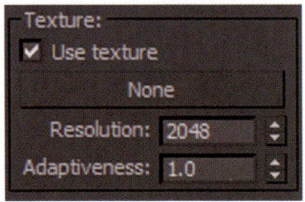

(8.11)

8.12

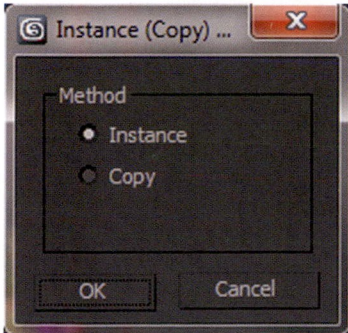

8.13

When the Instance (Copy) map pop up appears you need to select Instance and press OK. This is important because any changes you make to the HDRI will automatically be updated rather than having to drag and drop the HDRI into the light's properties again and again 8.13.

Almost there, stick with me it will be worth it!

Now we need to load the remaining large HDRI file into our scene to act as the background image.

As before select a blank material and import the HDRI_EVE_HIGH.hdr file from the same location. Make sure the Mapping Type is set to Spherical.

A final important part is telling Max to use this HDRI as a backdrop. Press 8 on your keyboard to open the Environment and Effects dialog.

Under the Common Parameters section you will see Background. Check the Use map to enable the texture rollout slot. Simply drag and drop the high-quality HDRI file from the Materials Editor to the empty slot in the Environment Map slot.

When the Instance (Copy) Map pop up appears, be sure to select Instance 8.14 .

Now we can start to concentrate on the artificial lighting in the form of V-Ray IES lights.

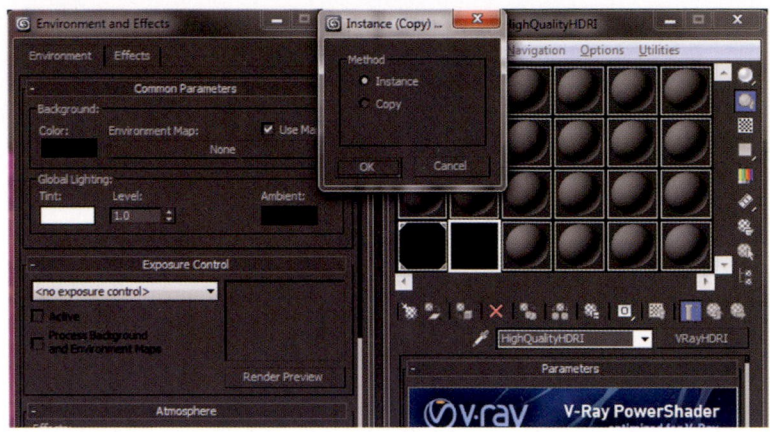

8.14

8.15

We need to create a photometric light that will cast realistic light and shadows onto our scene's geometry.

The photometric light creation tools can be found in the Create panel. Choose VRay from the drop down menu and in the object type select the VRayIES button 8.15.

Creating a light source is simple; drag and point. The first click is where you want to place the light source and the second click is the direction.

Try to align your lights correctly as per the ceiling layout. In the front and right viewport align the light vertically so that it points straight down. Here is my alignment 8.16.

The light source is in place and correctly aligned; now we need to adjust the properties to match real-world values.

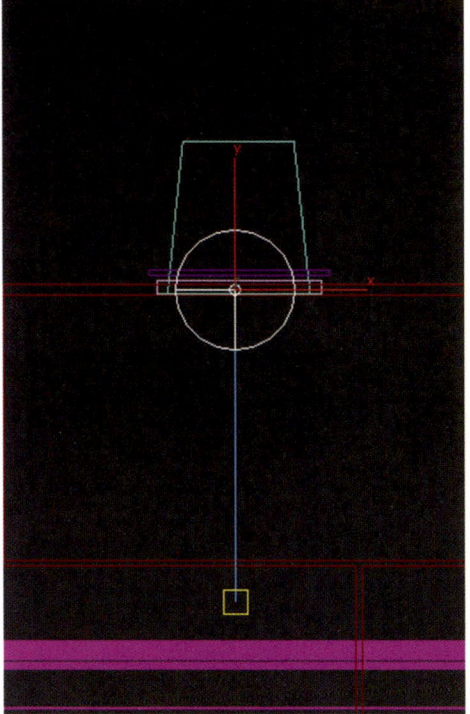

8.16

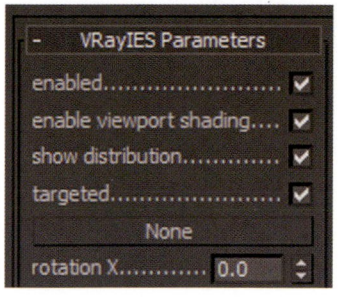

(8.17)

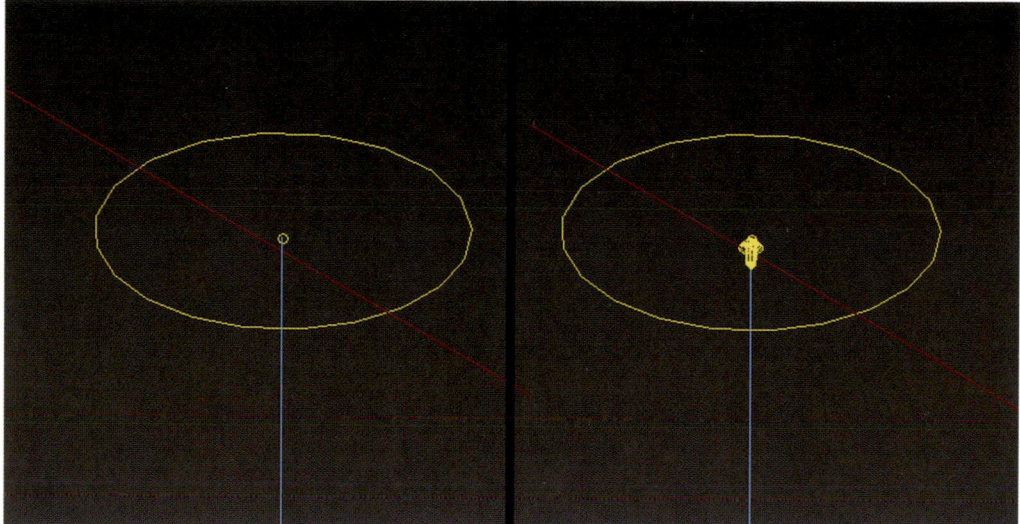

(8.18)

Luckily the majority of these settings will come from the manufacturer's IES file.

In the Modify panel you will see a group of settings that allow us to adjust the light. There is an empty slot with the name None. Go ahead and click this slot so thar we can load an IES file (8.17).

From the project folder load the IES file named 2782724. As soon as the file is loaded notice the emitter icon of your light change to match the settings of the IES. This is reflecting the real-world lighting fixtures attributes (8.18).

Now that we have a master IES light source, we need to copy this around the room and correctly align it to the remaining light fixtures. Be sure to instance copy the light otherwise you will have to manually adjust every single light individually when making changes.

Now we have the lights set up we can go ahead and set up the camera.

CAMERAS

You are probably wondering if this amount of camera work is really necessary. My answer is absolutely. Following this workflow will boost your understanding of how cameras work both indoors and outdoors. Your renders will be accurate and physically balanced, requiring minimal post-production.

When we use the HDRI method to light daytime exterior scenes, we can take advantage of the captured data and manipulate the cameras to achieve different moods.

Evening and nighttime HDRI lighting files however are much more delicate. They lack color temperature depth somewhat compared to daytime ones. What does this mean?

Well, it means as the HDRI environment is pretty much set, we have to be creative with the camera values to achieve a realistic shot. There may just be artificial captured lighting data from a light post or from a building embedded into the HDRI file. When the camera ISO is adjusted from a value of 100 to a value of 1600, these light emitters will affect the geometry in the scene, especially reflections, adding beautiful detail.

The downside to using a high ISO value in nighttime shots is that the image can be grainy or return overbright, so we have to adjust the other critical camera settings to even this out.

In our case we have many warm IES lights in the interior space which we want to emphasize with the camera.

As the human eye is light sensitive, it sees the warmest part of a picture first, so our emphasis on the interior space in an evening shot will be rather straightforward and produce seamless lighting conditions from cold to warm.

Create a V-Ray Physical Camera and place it in your scene. Try to place the camera so that you can pick up a portion of the environment around the building as well as capturing detail within the space (8.19).

I am going to share with you some fairly straightforward camera settings typical for nighttime photography. We can adjust them later if we do not like them.

With your camera selected go to the Modify panel and open up the camera's properties.

Go ahead and set the f-number to a value of 8.0.

Be sure to click the Guess vert.

Set the white balance to Daylight.

The shutter speed should be set to a value of around 4.3. You can play with this later in the render section.

(8.19)

targeted.............	✔
film gate (mm).......	75.0
focal length (mm)...	59.4
fov...............	☐ 64.262
zoom factor.........	1.0
horizontal offset....	0.0
vertical offset......	0.0
f-number............	8.0
target distance......	11483.
vertical shift........	0.137
horizontal shift......	0.0
Guess vert.	Guess horiz.
specify focus........	☐
focus distance.......	200.0
exposure............	✔
vignetting........	✔ 1.0
white balance	Daylight ▼
custom balance	
temperature.........	6500.0
shutter speed (s^-1	4.3
shutter angle (deg).	180.0
shutter offset (deg)	0.0
latency (s)..........	0.0
film speed (ISO).....	100.0

Finally adjust the film speed (ISO) to a value of 100.0.

Here is how the camera settings should look :

Now these are my settings that I have calculated and previously used on commercial projects. There are other ways and combinations for you to explore.

Now that we have the camera data inputted, we can set up the V-Ray settings.

V-RAY SETTINGS

The benefit of producing night renders is that the majority of the hard work comes from everything else other than the V-Ray settings.

In fact we do not need to deviate from the previous workflows for rendering the other scenes in this book with the exception of product rendering. With this is mind let's swiftly set up the V-Ray render parameters.

With the project exercise still open go ahead and press F10 on your keyboard to bring up the Render Setup window.

V-Ray is already enabled as the production renderer.

From the tabs at the top click on the V-Ray tab (8.21).

From the V-Ray:: Frame buffer rollout enable the built-in Frame Buffer. Make sure that the Get resolution from MAX is enabled (8.22).

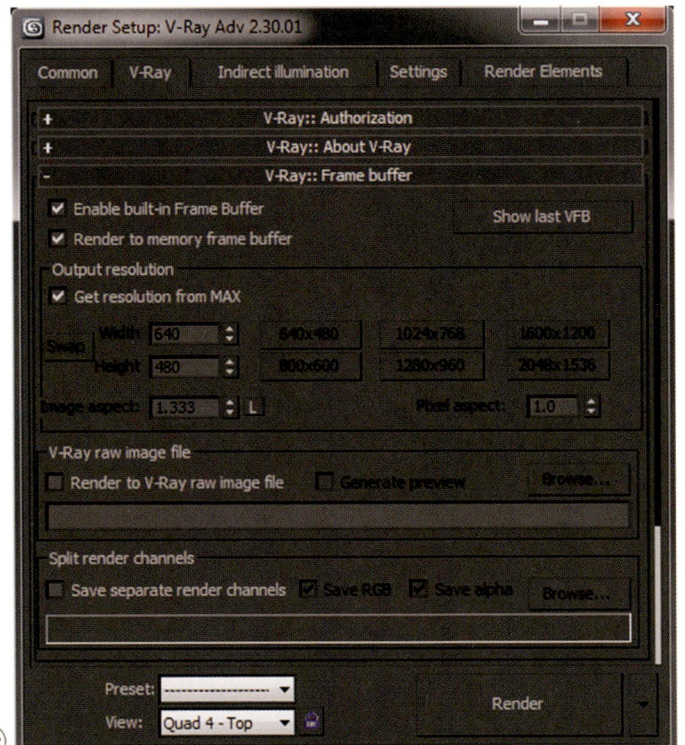

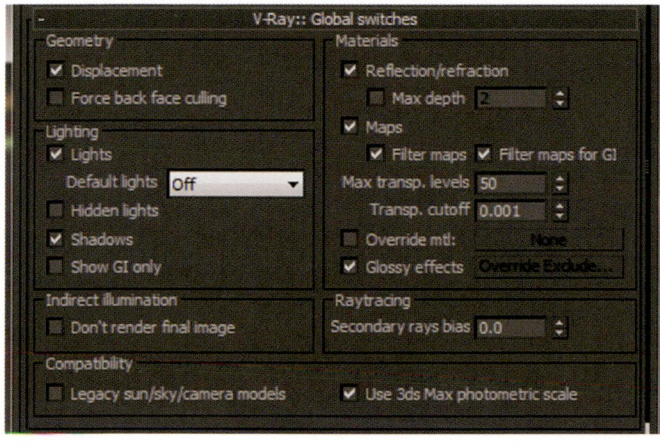

8.23

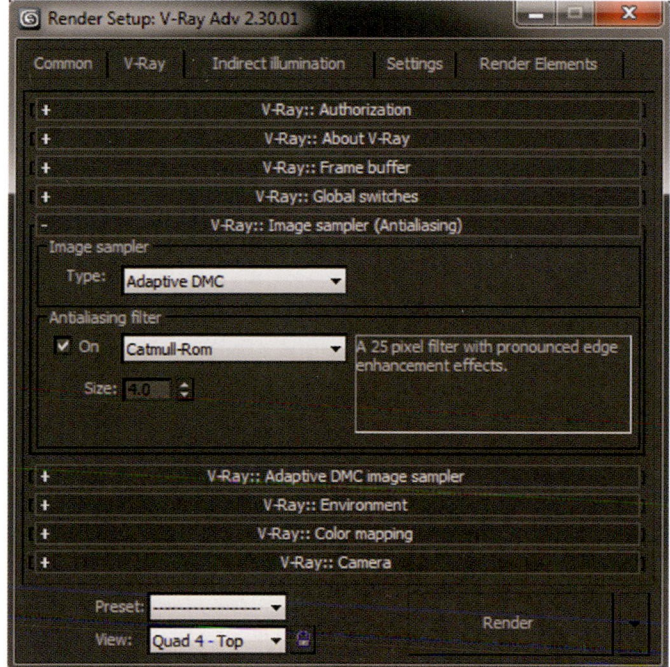

8.24

Next open the V-Ray:: Global switches rollout. In here un-check Hidden lights. Select Off from the Default lights drop down menu 8.23.

You should find the V-Ray:: Image sampler (Antialiasing) rollout just below the Global switches rollout.

In here change the Image sampler to Adaptive DMC from the drop down menu.

Due to the amount of detail in the geometry contained within this scene, I want V-Ray to emphasize all the hard work put into the model when rendering. To do this we will be using the Catmull-Rom filter. You can choose this from the drop down menu 8.24.

Scroll down to the V-Ray:: Color mapping rollout.

In the Type selection area choose Reinhard from the drop down menu. The evening HDRI does not contain as much color or temperature as the daytime HDRIS, so we do not need to use a low value to adjust the burn amount.

Furthermore the more you reduce the value of the Bright Multiplier the more you reduce the performance of the arti-ficial IES lights. So as you can imagine balancing the image out within Max is not so easy.

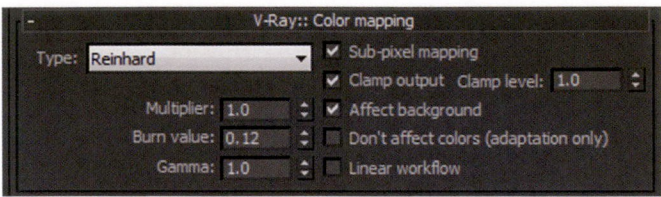

8.25

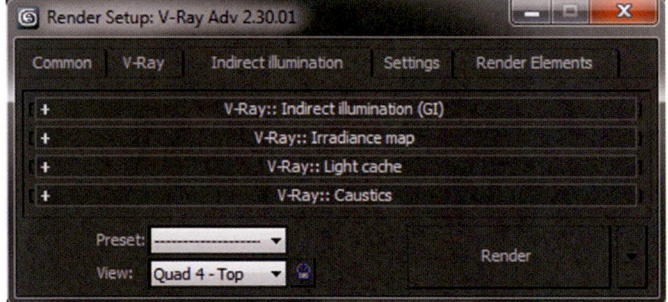

8.26

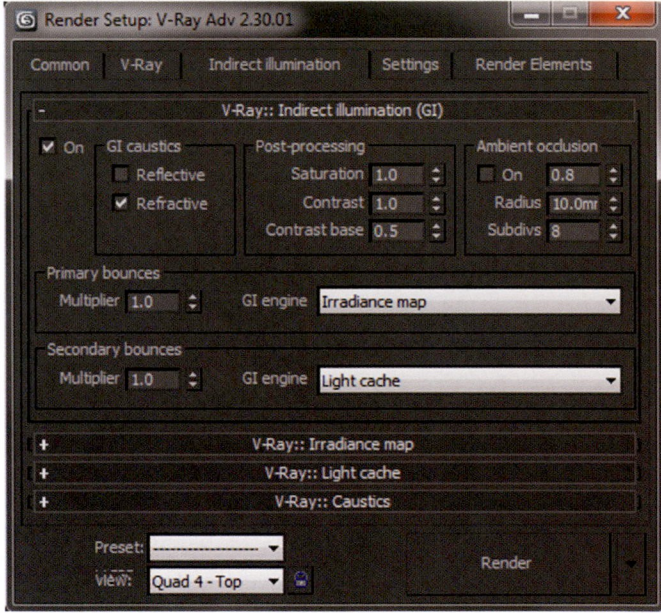

8.27

Now you have enabled Exponential as the type, go ahead and adjust the Bright multiplier to a value of 0.5. Make sure that Sub-pixel mapping, Clamp output and Affect background are all enabled 8.25.

Back to the top of the F10 Render Setup dialog box, open up the Indirect Illumination tab 8.26.

In the V-Ray:: Indirect illumination rollout make sure that the On is enabled.

In the Primary bounces section set the GI engine to Irradiance map. Now set the Secondary bounces GI engine to Light cache 8.27.

In the V-Ray:: Irradiance map rollout there is a section named Built-in presets. From the drop down menu choose High. In the Options area just below make sure that Show calc. phase is enabled 8.28.

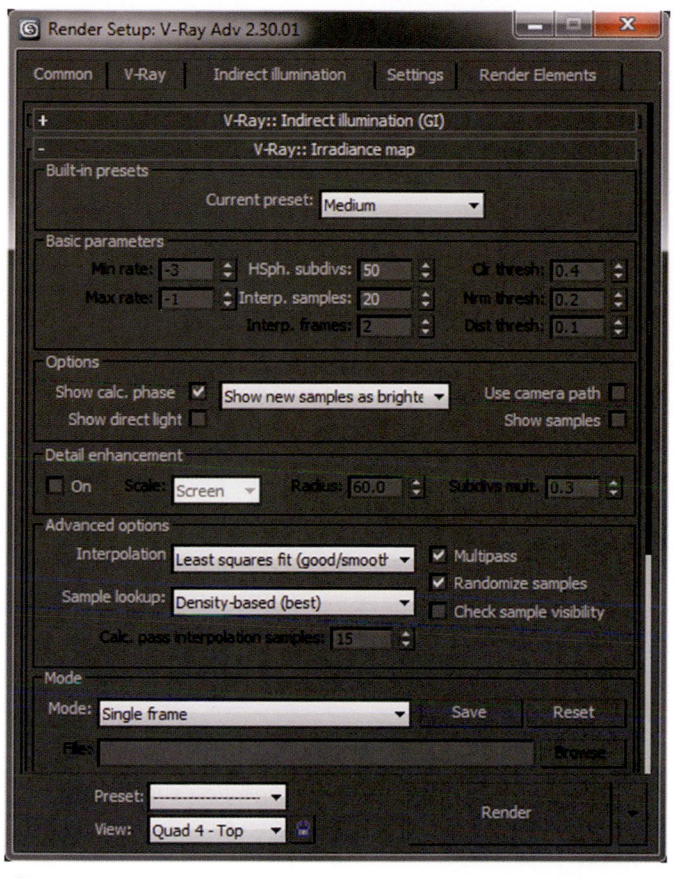

(8.28)

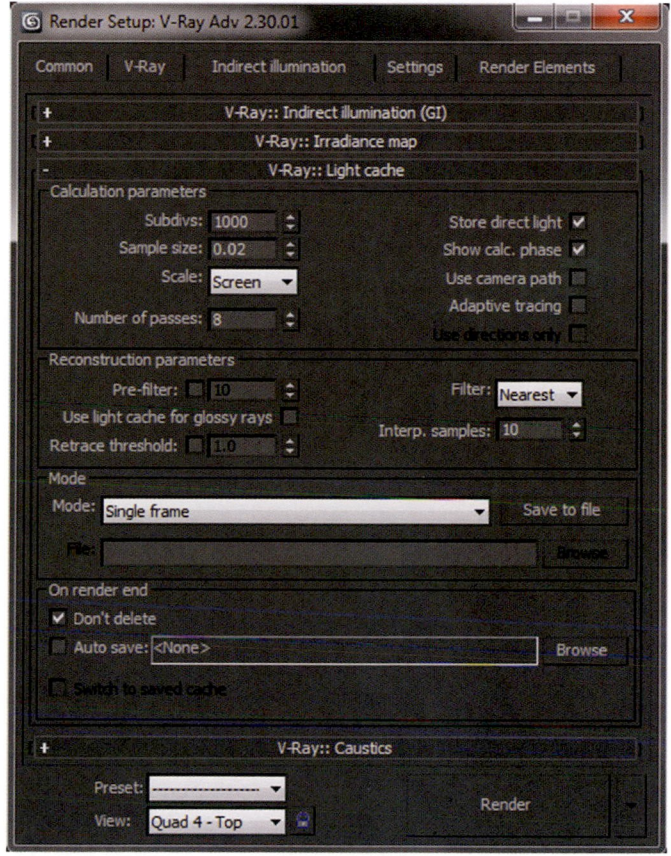

(8.29)

Just underneath open the V-Ray:: Light cache rollout. In here we need to input sufficient settings in order to render a quality scene.

As a general rule, bearing in mind that we need to stick to fast render times, in the Calculation parameters I set the Subdivs to equal 50 percent of my output render size. So for example the width of the render we will produce is 1920.

Fifty percent of this is 960, so we can enter a value of 960–1000. In this case you can input 1000. Keep the sample size set to 0.02. We want to instantly see the results as the render screen builds so enable Show calc. phase on the right (8.29).

Now we have the majority of the base settings set up.

Like everything in design, when you are replicating reality in a digital format, there are always tweaks to be made.

Now you can proceed to the rendering stage.

RENDERING

I always like to render an exterior evening shot with and without artificial lights. Let's take a look at how the scene would look without IES lights (8.30).

It is a nice effect. You can see that the HDRI is really effective, casting moonlight tones on the aluminum cladding. More importantly the glazing is really performing as it should.

(8.30)

Let's now take a look at the final rendered output with all lights enabled and active (8.31).

The IES lights are performing as they should without any significant unrealistic burning effects. The warm light is certainly prominent in the reflections of the aluminum cladding that wraps around the external envelope of the space, acting as a buffer between natural and artificial light.

The reflections in the glazing elements are still performing and correctly showing slight double reflections due to the double glazing.

I am happy with this scene. There may be some slight room for post-production work; however I would use this as is for client approval.

Now you can adjust the camera ISO to see what alternating the values gives you in visual feedback. Try the same for the f-stop and shutter speed. You can also use the guide in the photography section in Chapter 10 for alternate camera settings.

CHAPTER 9

AUTOMOTIVE SCENES

DESIGN PROCESS

Transportation design is a field that I have always been interested in. I can remember when I first watched the Citroën C4 advert on television. I was blown away with the realistic lighting and materials applied to the transforming car.

When the movie *Transformers* was released it blew my mind. It remains to this day the best movie for visual effects in my opinion.

As my career has progressed I have become increasingly aware of how important 3D skills are and the potential markets that one can go into with such skills.

In this section of the book I want to open your minds. I want you to see the potential you can achieve using V-Ray and the built-in materials and lighting tools available to you.

There are many talented digital artists out there who can build the 3D meshes of any vehicle from a simple front, side and top blueprint of a vehicle (9.1).

On the other hand there are those of us out there who cannot dedicate the time to build such realistic and accurate 3D models, so we look elsewhere. There are numerous online outlets where you can purchase a fully scaled and already textured 3D mesh of a vehicle. Check the companion website for links to these resources.

For more information on this topic, please visit
WWW.FOCALPRESS.COM/CW/WYLDE!

For this chapter's supporting exercise you will be creating a photoshoot scene similar to those that appear in the glossy motorsport magazines.

In this scene I have provided you with one Pontiac Solstice. Let's go ahead and take a look at the scene.

 9.1

LIGHTING

As we are creating a shoot similar to what you would see in a product brochure or magazine, we can set up the lighting to best suit the chosen format.

We will be creating a backdrop like you would get in a commercial photoshoot as well as the key lights (9.2).

(9.2)

Open the scene file **09_Transportation_Start.max** from the project folder.

Here is a quick snapshot of the scene (9.3).

This is an incredibly simple scene. I have created a backdrop to simulate a canvas if you will. The vehicle is positioned accordingly so as to not show the edges of the backdrop.

The lighting method we will use will simulate studio lights as illustrated in Figure 9.2

To do this we will need to use the V-Ray light toolsets. Mimicking realistic light levels is essential otherwise the product will not be correctly displayed in all its glory. Chances are the client will not be happy either if you have been commissioned to produce such visuals.

We will now go ahead and create three V-Ray plane lights.

In the lighting creation panel drag and drop a VRay Plane Light into the top viewport (9.4).

 9.3

9.4

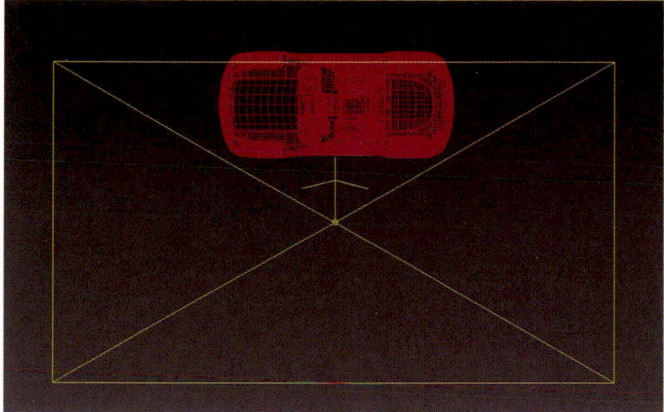

(9.5)

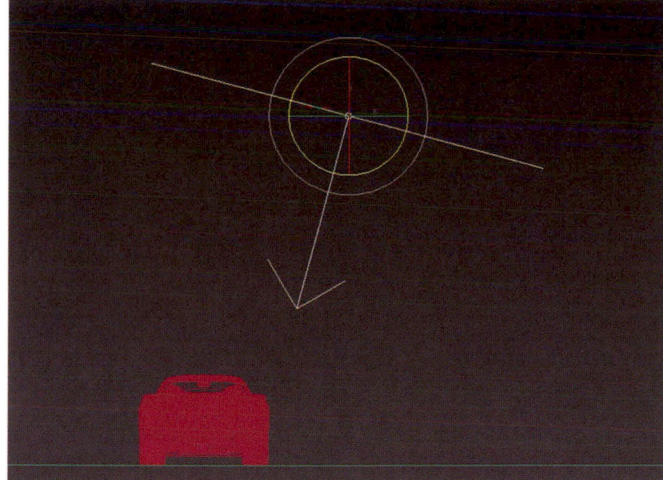

(9.6)

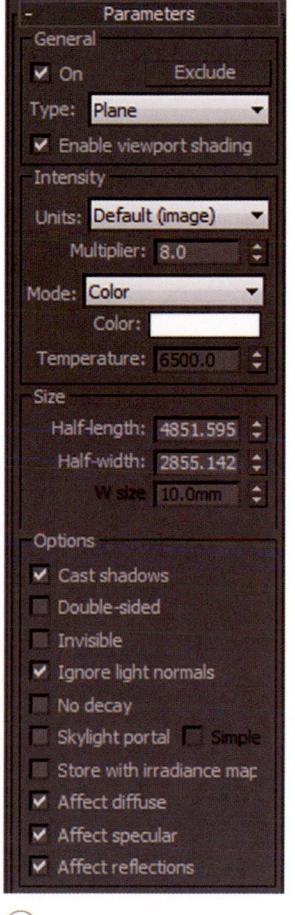

(9.7)

Make sure that the light covers a significant portion of the vehicle in order to illuminate it properly; here is where I placed mine (9.5).

We now need to rotate the light so that we can maximize the rectilinear reflections on the vehicle's curved surfaces (9.6).

Once you have done this you can go ahead and set the light's properties to match the following (9.7).

I would like you now to make two more lights such as you have previously created. Place each light as shown (9.8).

This scene would look pretty flat if we simply made all the light emit a white color of 255,255,255. Instead we can add a gradient type light effect by adjusting the color coming in from the left and right by adjusting the color settings.

The light emitting from the left-hand side of the screen should be less powerful than the rest.

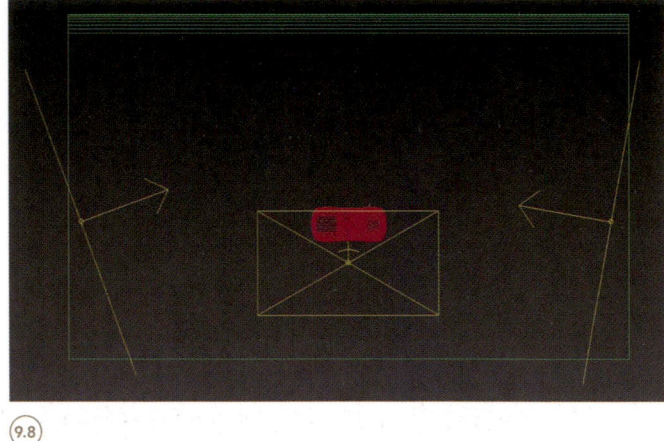

(9.8)

Go ahead and change the settings of this light to match (9.9).

Now let's go ahead and change the light coming from the right-hand side of the scene to be a daylight type temperature with a higher value so that the shadow-casting changes to add increased depth to the scene. Change the light's settings to match (9.10).

Now you have the lights set up you can proceed to create the cameras and finalize the scene's settings.

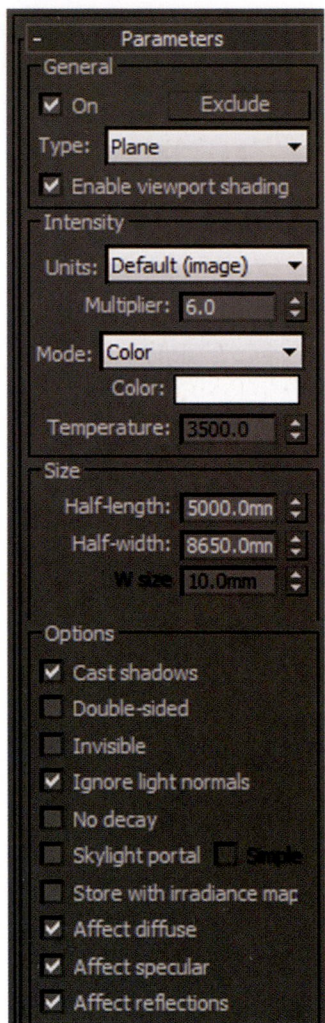

(9.9)

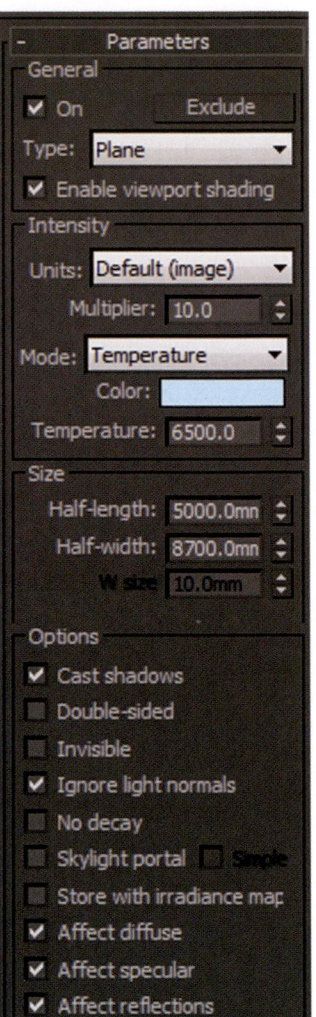

(9.10)

CAMERAS

For this scene I want you to use the normal standard 3D Studio Max Camera. We have already used V-Ray Physical Cameras throughout this book.

In the interests of diversity I believe you should see what type of results can be achieved utilizing alternative cameras.

With your scene open go to the top viewport. I want you to create a camera from the Standard camera panel and place it looking directly at the backdrop and the side elevation of the vehicle 9.11.

9.12 shows where I placed my camera.

One of the great features of the built-in 3D Studio Max Standard Camera is that you can simply select a stock lens and you are instantly updated in the viewport with the result. Unlike V-Ray Physical Cameras there are no exposure settings etc. to fiddle with; this is a straight point-and-shoot method.

9.11

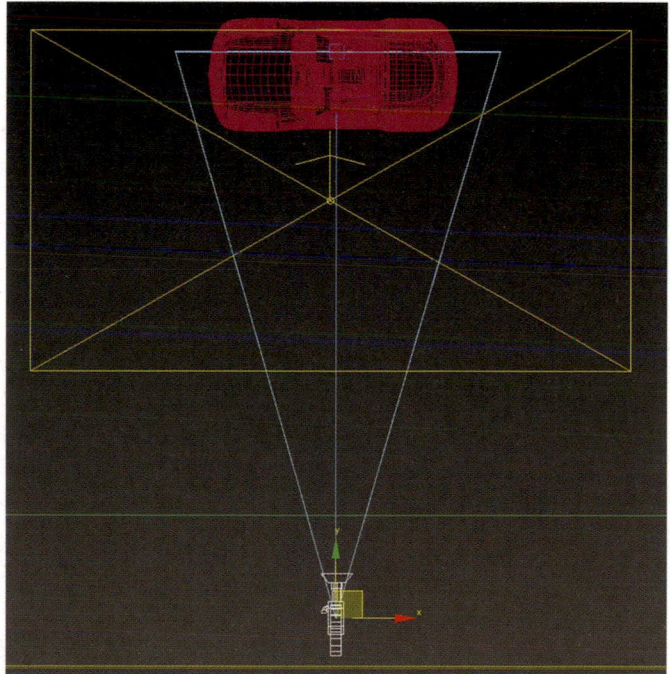

9.12

Press C on your keyboard and go to your camera view. You will need to raise the camera in the Z direction to achieve a suitable result. The image below shows how my camera is placed (9.13).

Finally with your camera selected, go to the properties toolset and scroll down to the section called Multi-Pass Effect.

From the drop down menu select Depth of Field. Also make sure the Enable is checked (9.14).

Now you have completed the majority of the hard work, we can now proceed and finalize the render settings and see what type of output we are presented with.

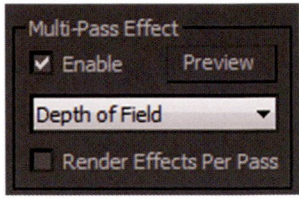

(9.14)

(9.13)

V-RAY SETTINGS

As with the rest of the scenes you should be used to the generic setup by now.

As this is essentially a product scene, we will need the main V-Ray settings to be primarily focused on outlining the surface detail of the vehicle and correctly calculating color and tone etc.

Open up your file from the point of last saving.

Press F10 on your keyboard. The usual Render dialog should appear 9.15.

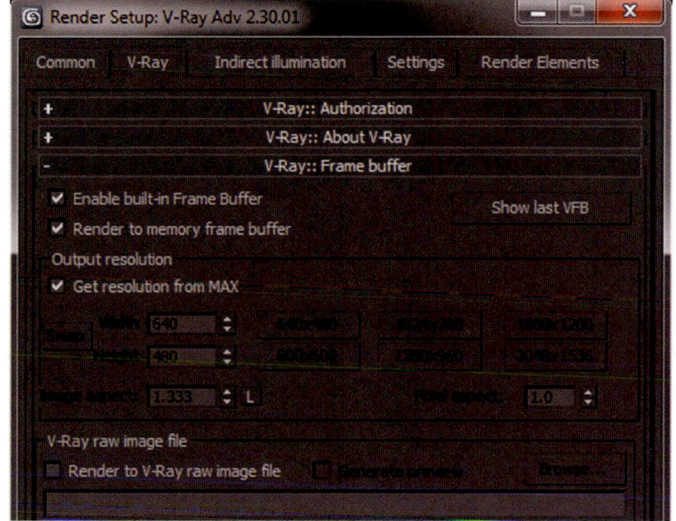

9.16

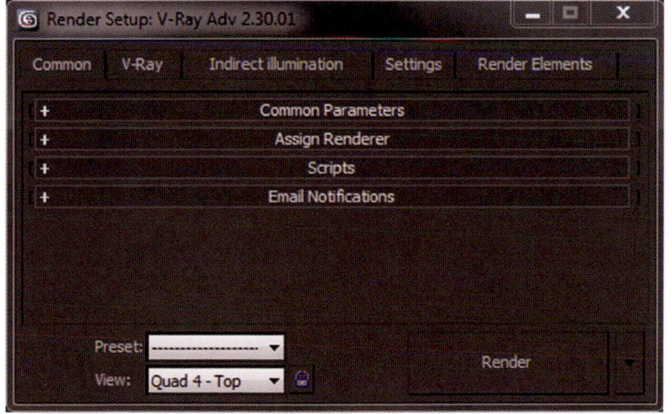

9.15

From the V-Ray tab at the top direct your way to the V-Ray :: Frame buffer tab. Make sure the settings are as shown in 9.16.

Next scroll down to the V-Ray:: Global switches tab. In here you need to match the settings as shown (over) 9.17.

Just below you will see V-Ray:: Image sampler. Enter the values as shown 9.18.

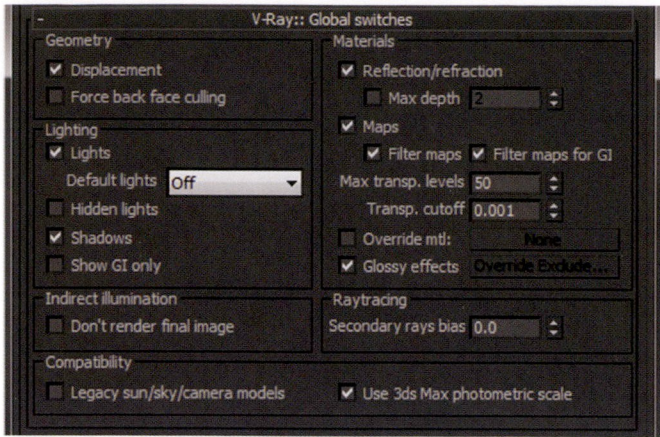

9.17

9.19

9.20

9.18

Next we need to adjust the color mapping so that we avoid any undue burning. Even though we are not utilizing the HDRI lighting method, artificial lights can still return over-bright areas and damage the scene's realistic output. Scroll down to the V-Ray:: Color mapping rollout. Make sure that the settings are as shown 9.19 .

Next we need to enable the Global illumination methods. At the top of the F10 pop up window, select the next tab called Indirect Illumination. In the first rollout in this section set the Primary and Secondary bounces to match 9.20 .

Below adjust the V-Ray:: Irradiance map settings to mimic those shown 9.21 .

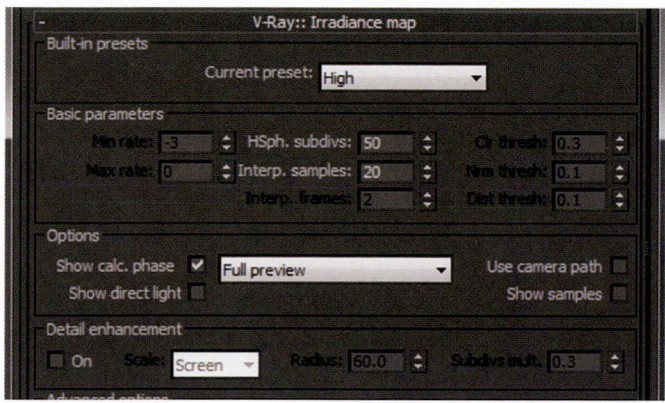

(9.21)

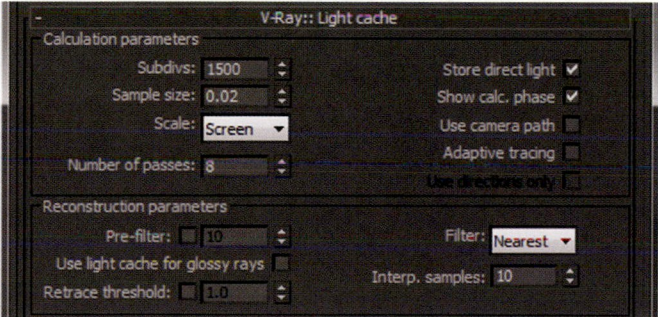

(9.22)

Finally in the V-Ray:: Light cache rollout, copy the settings in (9.22) to complete the final stages of the render settings.

Now we can render the scene.

RENDERING

This is a fairly basic scene yet has incredibly realistic results. Go ahead and press F9 on your keyboard to product a final render.

You will notice that the scene keeps rendering. This is because we have the Multi-Pass Effect switched on which is the Depth of Field.

The final result is rather nice (9.23).

You can now explore even further with your own creative methods of lighting.

CHAPTER 10

SHOOTING HDRIS

INTRODUCTION

Throughout this book I refer to HDRI or HDR files; in fact they make up most of the workflow when lighting the scenes in each of the exercises (10.1).

This chapter adopts a more practical approach to creating your own photographic back plates for your 3D scenes to enable them to function as lighting and environment subject matter.

It is incredibly beneficial for you to have alternative custom HDRI files for your library. Many designers search the far corners of the internet to try and download free ones but nothing really compares with utilizing your own skills to complete the full workflow and deliver quality.

I know that there is a lot to learn in V-Ray and 3D Studio Max alone without having to educate yourself further with in-depth photography terms and workflows, but I promise you that if you pick this up and can effectively use this workflow from start to finish, then your work will be recognized and you will increase your employment potential.

The main ethos of this section of the book is to open your minds to experimental photography merged with 3D visualization. This section is meant to be fun so that you are not sat at a computer; to get you out on the ground, on site if you will, to become increasingly aware of the surroundings that the building or space you are visualizing will one day inhabit. Ultimately, it gets you out of the office!

(10.1)

METHODOLOGY

We are going to create one 3D Studio Max scene set up with V-Ray lighting to utilize the back plates we have photographed and the HDRI file we have created. The exercise should yield the following result (10.2) .

(10.2)

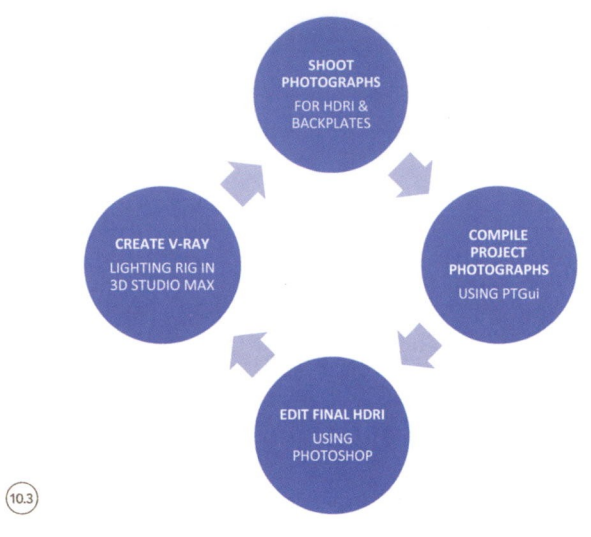

(10.3)

Usually when shooting panoramic images one would take perhaps five or six photographs in total while turning 360 degrees making sure that there is a sufficient overlap. The next stage would be to merge the photographs in Photoshop to create one final panoramic image.

While this would be an OK method, the final image file would be useless to use because it will not perform in the way we want it to as per this book's exercises.

We need a HDRI instead which contains the juicy lighting data that will realistically illuminate your scene's geometry.

To do this instead of shooting one image and then spinning the camera around, we will be taking three photographs in the same position and will then proceed to rotate the camera and do the same. This is bracketing.

To make your workflow easy to follow and to see the design process involved, here is a broad illustration outlining the process that we will follow (10.3).

In this exercise we are going to be shooting a series of photographs using a technique referred to as bracketing.

Bracketing is the general technique of taking several shots of the same subject using different camera settings.

Fundamentally we are going to photograph a series of images that will be shot in a rotational turn and then we will merge them together in stitching software called PTGui to create one large HDRI lighting file (10.4).

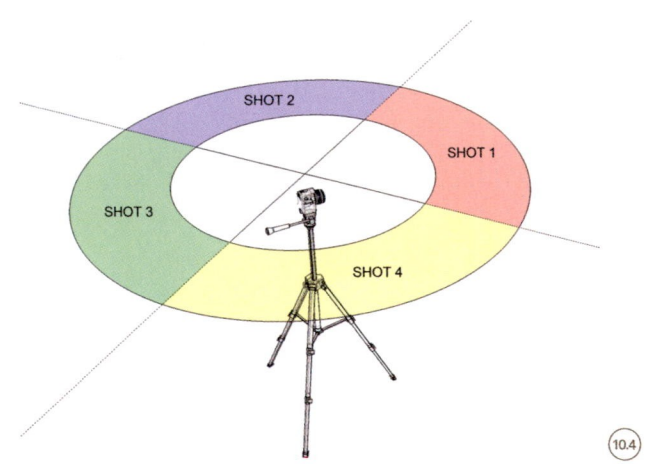

(10.4)

Each of the three photographs will be shot in the same position at alternate exposures. To put this simply, one image will be shot as per normal conditions, one will be overexposed and one will be underexposed.

Here is one sample of a bracketed image from the panorama in this exercise highlighting the three captured exposures (10.5).

It is the lighting information contained within these three images that once merged with each other can be used within V-Ray to achieve realistic lighting through the use of a V-Ray HDRI Power Shader.

We will need to use a mixture of Photoshop and a program called PTGui to compile the bracketed photographs we will be shooting, but it is minimal and actually straightforward.

(10.5)

Photoshop has some great tools to aid us with this workflow such as HDR toning and the ability to make refinements. PTGui is an incredible piece of software that super stream-lines the HDR merging process. It does take some time to process, usually around 20 minutes, but it is well worth the wait!

This sounds rather in-depth and to some a little too much, however once you complete your first shoot you'll be up and running in no time and wanting to create more.

The greater and more varied collection of HDRIS you possess, the more flexible you can be with the final quality of the renders you produce.

CHOOSING A LOCATION

First of all you should be able to get there! If you have to watch *Mission Impossible* the night before to help you venture out for your shoot, then it is not worth it!

There is no point risking your safety to capture a HDRI. You may as well spend $30 purchasing one that looks similar.

Depending on which type of mood you want to achieve in your V-Ray scene, you should plan a trip that takes advantage of the best possible natural lighting conditions.

I am in Dubai and now it is almost summertime I am slowly seeing the beautiful bright blue sky turn yellow and hazy due to the humidity. This will significantly affect my HDRI and ultimately the feel of my scene (10.6).

I often try to shoot at midday if I am producing daytime renders. This means I can easily make use of the almost vertical shadows cast by the sun which emits directly over the camera.

This also helps with regard to adding and positioning a V-Ray Sun to cast proper shadows to match the chosen back plate.

I try to avoid anything in my HDRIS that will cause problems in the stitching software later on when compiling the final photographed panorama.

People and vehicles are a nuisance; you have to wait for them to move.

The ocean is another problem due to the waves never staying still in time for you to do a full 180 or 360 degree shoot.

If you are producing interior visuals then some of these issues are not really relevant as your primary focus is within the 3D Studio Max scene, so you can rotate the HDRI to avoid seeing those captured issues that you do not want visible.

All in all, the HDR file is simply for light casting and reflections; your back plate will be the main image that you want to perfect as it will be visible to the camera.

EQUIPMENT

In order to successfully capture the projects HDR, you are going to require some basic equipment. I used my wife's Canon 550D for this exercise (10.7).

Usually I use my 450D but the quality of the image is far superior using the 550D. It is a great camera and is not too complicated to operate. You can easily adjust the settings and it lends itself well to this kind of practical work.

I use a basic tripod so there is no need to go out and purchase an expensive solution.

(10.8)

(10.7)

One note on tripods: if you are going to purchase a new one, make sure you test it first in the store. Sometimes the legs can be rather flimsy and the rotation not very smooth. Some tripods do not come with spirit levels built in so you have to be sure that this will work for you.

It is important to try and purchase a tripod with a tiltable head so that you can place your camera at 90 degrees (portrait) as well as 180 degrees (landscape). Again this depends on what type of scene you want to capture.

You can get around this by purchasing some mounting plates instead; a simple 90 degree mount can do the job .

For our purposes in this book, it would not be practical to spend significant amounts on mounts etc, so for this exercise we will stick to a good old tripod and mount the camera as normal.

Try to have plenty of storage available on your memory cards. I use a 4 GB card for every project; it makes it easy to track the files down and not delete my wife's pictures!

Take two batteries. Shooting HDRIS can put stress on your camera processing multiple photographs so you need to make sure that you are not stuck in the middle of a field shouting and swearing because your battery went after only the first set of bracketed shots. I have done this before.

Finally we want to be nowhere near the camera while it is capturing the scene. To get around this I use a $10 remote for the Canon camera (10.9).

(10.9)

This enables me to simply turn the camera to certain angles and then move out of the way so I am not casting shadows on the floor within the camera's view and so I am not visible in any reflections once in Max.

Not touching the camera is important; any change in the position other than on its rotational axis could affect the final merged panorama and how it is generated.

PREPARATION

Should you mount your camera horizontally or vertically? The answer is how much work do you want to do and what type of result are you looking for?

Ideally you need to capture as much of the sky as possible together with foreground. If you do not do this correctly then your panorama will look squashed in your reflections as below (10.10).

If you shoot the scene using your camera in a normal position (landscape) then you may need to take many more photographs to make up the shortfall for sky etc.

If on the other hand you use your camera rotated 90 degrees (portrait) then you will capture much more detail with a vertical emphasis. You will however have to shoot more photographs to make up the 360 degree panorama.

I will highlight the differences between the two orientation methods of shooting later. For now we need to work out the camera settings so that we can proceed with the shoot.

The easiest way to figure out what the best settings are for your scene wherever in the world you are is to take a photograph with your camera set to full auto mode. Then you can simply input those values into your camera in manual mode. Here are the settings for my chosen destination (10.11).

So now I will go ahead and program the ISO, shutter speed and f-number into my camera.

In order to shoot this correctly we need to close off or lock some of the other settings so that the camera does not automatically calculate things such as focus, white balance etc.

If you are shooting a panoramic scene with multiple shots and your camera is not set to manual then the final merged panoramic HDRI will vary in focus and in white balance in certain parts and produce unrealistic results in V-Ray.

So with that in mind we will now set up the camera to eliminate any fluctuations between photographs.

Looking through your viewfinder, zoom out as much as you can to capture items such as the top of trees, buildings, lights etc. I am using a Cannon 10–22mm lens.

Here is what I can see through my viewfinder (10.12).

The image is well proportioned to obtain sufficient foreground coverage as well as background depth and to display enough sky.

Perhaps most importantly the horizon is in the center of the image as it should be, always try and position the horizon line in the middle of your photographs. This is because when you put your final HDRI into 3D Studio Max, if the horizon line is offset in any way in the captured photographs then it will be off in 3D Studio Max also, so your lighting will return incorrectly balanced and positioned, negatively affecting reflections etc.

Now I can proceed to finalize my settings. I am firstly going to lock off my white balance by setting it to daylight in manual mode (10.13).

Next I am going to switch from Auto focus to Manual focus, making sure I do not alter the focus from now until I am finished with the shoot (10.14).

10.14

10.15

10.13

I now need to tell the camera that I want to take multiple exposures. To do this I must access the camera's menu (10.15).

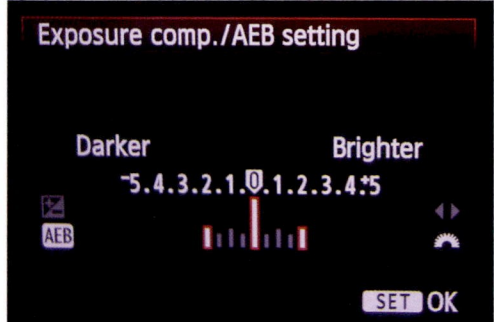

I navigate my way to the Expo.comp./AEB menu option. With this selected I simply scroll the function wheel to the right so that the settings look like this .

Finally I need to instruct the camera to use continuous shooting mode as the method of capture. This means when I press the remote a series of three images will be shot one after the other.

Now that the camera is set up, I then make sure that the coast is clear and start shooting. Like I said previously it is

better to shoot fast as it avoids any unwanted visitors in your HDR files.

The shooting method is fairly simple, the general rule is to try and get a 30 percent overlap between camera rotations. Remember if you are shooting with your camera rotated at 90 degrees (portrait) then you will be taking a lot more photographs than in landscape orientation.

With my bracketed photographs complete I then decide on what type of backplate shot I will require.

If for instance I am rendering a product or vehicle, then I will try and take some shots that emphasize the product's curves or details so that they can be viewed in proportion with the backplate.

Normally designers will shoot a high resolution photograph in JPEG format for their backplates. I like to use the bracketing method. Why? Simply because I want more control when matching my HDRI lighting to my backplate.

You can really push the boundaries of HDR photography utilizing V-Ray. Having said this if you want straightforward JPEGs then this is fine also, it totally depends on timeframe and ultimately the project in hand and what you are comfortable with (10.19).

So now with the shoot complete we can focus on the collation, processing and compiling of the HDRI files.

COMPILING HDRIS

Now we are ready to actually make the HDRI lighting file and as such I suggest creating a new project folder on your desktop to keep track of the files.

You can download a free trial of PTGui from www.ptgui. com which will install in seconds.

Once installed go ahead and launch the program .

PTGui is a pretty simple interface and incredibly easy to use. Let me just fill you in on one of the normal HDRI creation methods.

Many designers load each shot of three bracketed photographs into Adobe Photoshop and use the Merge to HDR Pro function to form each rotational image.

This is a rather time-consuming method of creating the HDRIS and at the end of the process you will have a number of individual HDR files that will still need stitching together.

Photoshop cannot stitch HDR files using its automated tool set named Photomerge.

This is why I find it essential to introduce you to PTGui. It eradicates long-winded workloads utilizing in Photoshop.

Let's go ahead and produce the HDRI panorama.

Click the 1.Load images… button .

10.20

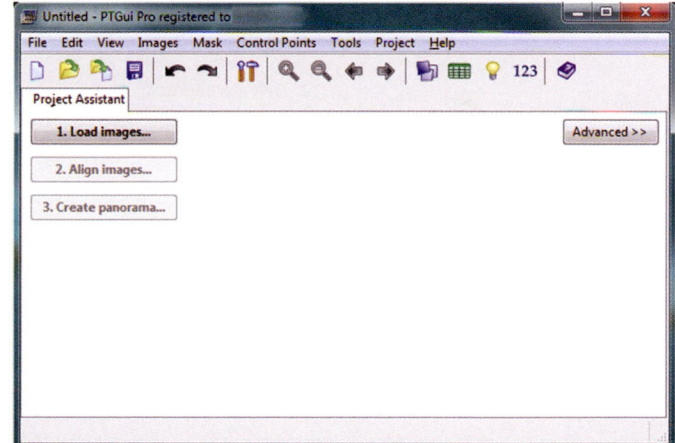

10.21

Browse to the folder you have created on your desktop that contains the photographed bracketed images.

Try not to mix your backplates with the panorama ones! Create a different folder so that you can keep a track on them.

Select all the bracketed images and then click Open (10.22).

Once loaded you will see all of your bracketed photographs have loaded in a linear display (10.23).

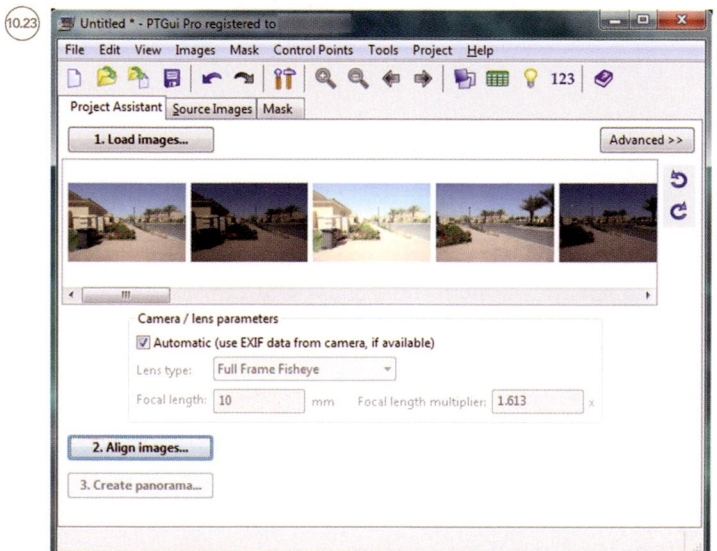

Next we need to tell the program to process all the images, merge them into HDR files and then show us the overlapped HDR panorama. Go ahead and click the 2. Align Images… button.

Now you will notice a Bracketed Exposures menu appear, fear not as our selection process is very straightforward (10.24).

We need to instruct PTGui to Enable HDR mode and to link the HDR files as we shot them using the tripod.

This great piece of software informs you of the actions of selecting each option.

Finally we need to make sure the HDR method is set to true HDR (10.25).

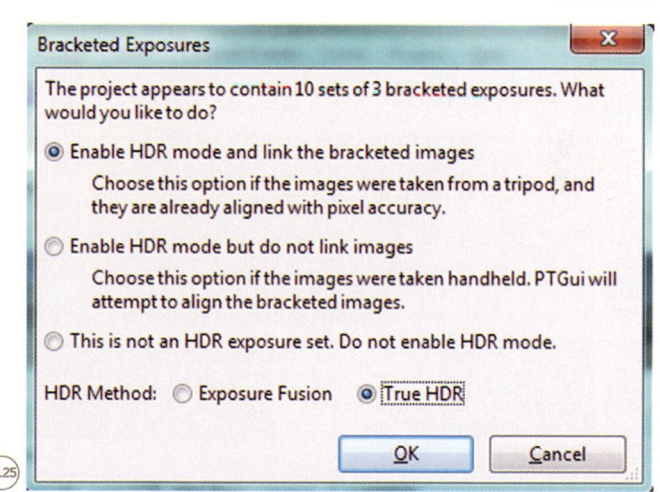

Once you have done this press the OK button and let the software do its thing .

If all has gone to plan then you should be presented with a large format panorama in a new window.

This interface enables you to view the merged bracketed photographs and how they have been stitched. You can change the method of mapping from spherical to cylindrical etc. For now just leave the settings as they are. You can experiment later .

The final stage in this process is to direct PTGui to finalize the images and create the HDR file.

Flick back to the main PTGui window. In here you will need to click on the 3. Create panorama… button (10.28).

The software will automatically give you the width and height based on the pre-captured and merged photographic data.

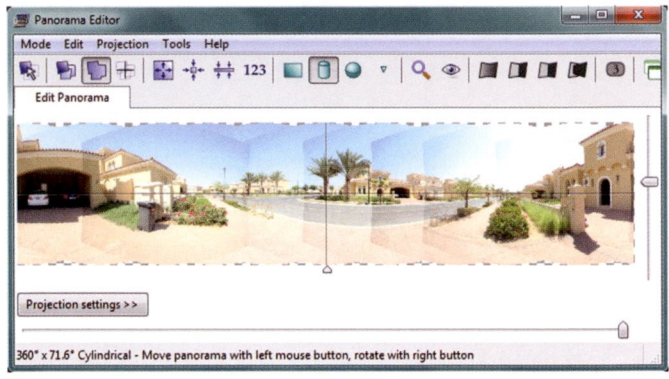

(10.27)

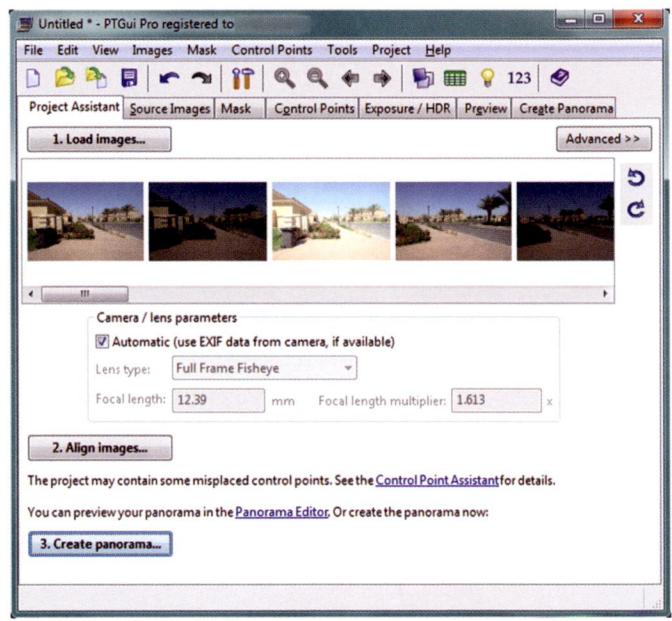

(10.28)

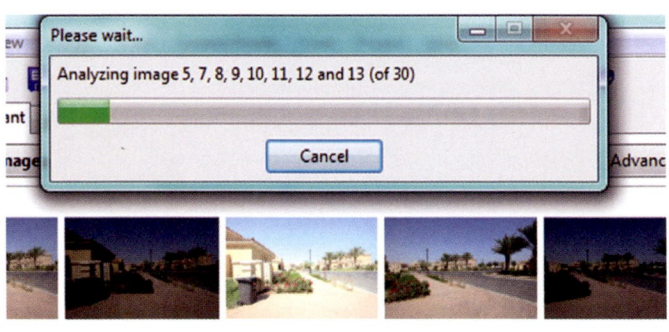

(10.26)

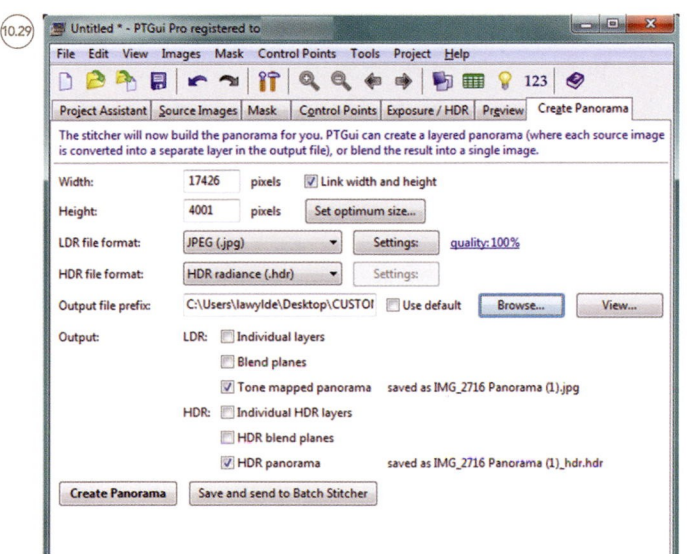

PTGui will give you two files, an LDR and a HDR. You already know what a HDR is, an LDR is a low dynamic range image and is often used as backplates. For us it is simply a preview image.

You can leave the settings as they are. Make sure that your output file path is set up to navigate to your desktop project folder.

Finally in the Output section make sure that your settings resemble the following 10.29.

You can now click the Create Panorama button.

Now may be a good time to make a cup of tea as the process will take around 10–20 minutes dependent on your hardware.

Once the process is complete you can view the files in the project folder. No need to open the HDR as there will be a JPEG file showing you the final result 10.30.

Now before we jump into 3D Studio Max and set up the V-Ray lighting, we need to adjust the HDR file so that the color, tone and exposure are looking sufficient to return a realistic result.

Using Photoshop we will now open up and edit the HDR file. Bear in mind that these files can be up to 200 MB in size and can take quite some time to save dependent on your system.

Notice the dark parts at the top and bottom of the image. This is due to the stitching method and the way the images have been overlapped. It is perfectly normal. All we have to do is crop the image to omit these defects. Alternatively you can use the stamp tool to fill the black parts with sky and any ground coverage (10.31).

Photoshop has some great tools for adjusting the quality and ultimately the performance of the HDR file. If you navigate your way to the menu header Image, you will see a subselection option named Adjustments. In here select the HDR Toning option (10.32).

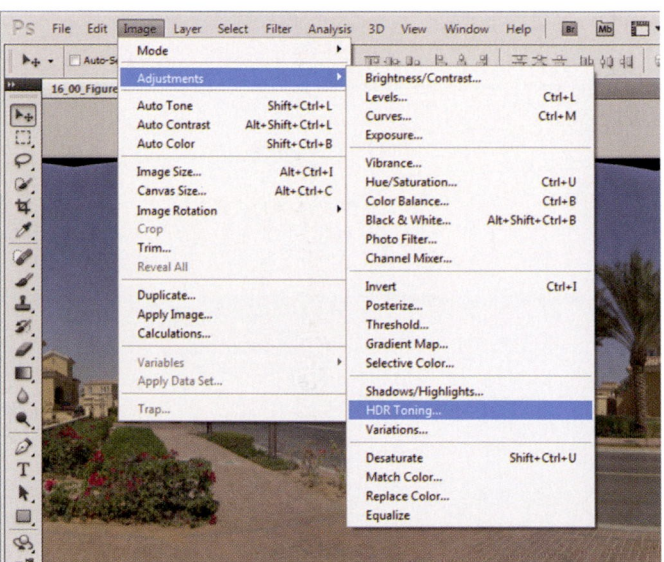

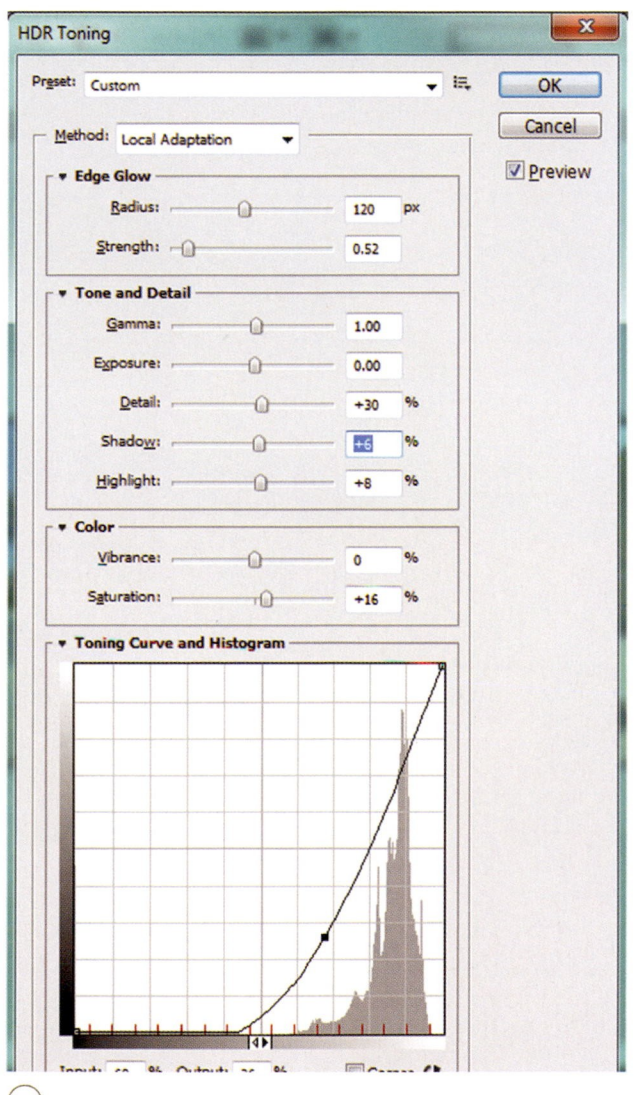

You will notice the subtle change to your HDR file when the HDR Toning menu loads. I tend to stick with the Local Adaptation method to tweak my HDRs. You can simply adjust the Tone and Detail values to suit your requirements. I also like to use the Histogram tool at the bottom so that I can control the results thorough the custom curves (10.33).

Once you are happy with the overall preview image simply click OK. It may take up to 30 seconds to apply the changes to the HDR file.

Now that you have the HDR lighting file ready for use we will now prepare the backplate.

As I mentioned before many designers simply use a JPEG to act as their backplate when producing V-Ray renders. My issue with this is ultimately performance. If I am adjusting the tone of my HDR lighting file, then I want my backplate to perform in the same fashion.

The first thing to do is to make sure that you have your bracketed backplate files ready for processing. Shown (over) is my backplate without any modification (10.34).

I used PTGui previously to compile the bracketed photographs and to ultimately form the panoramic HDR.

Since I only need to create one HDR and not a series, this time I am going to show you the process of compiling the HDR in Adobe Photoshop.

Open up Adobe Photoshop.

We will use the simple process of a built-in feature in Photoshop to merge the files. Navigate your way to File, then go to Automate, and then select the Merge to HDR Pro… option (10.35).

A pop up menu will appear and from this you can simply press the Browse button.

Now select the three bracketed photographs and press Open (10.36).

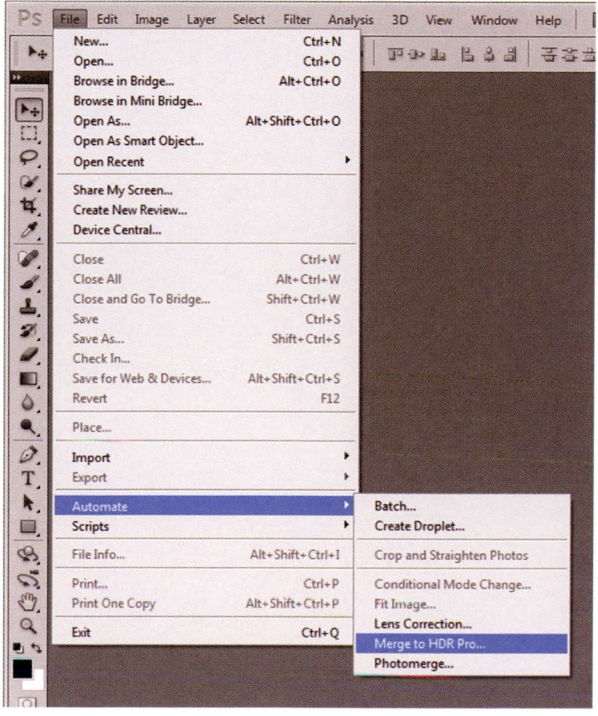

10.35

10.36

10.37

All you have to do now is to make sure that the Attempt to Automatically Align Source Images is checked. Next press OK.

Let Photoshop do its thing; it should take around 20 seconds. All that is happening is the blending and overlapping of each image.

Once ready you should see the following screen .

Take note of the three bracketed exposures at the bottom of the screen. Notice the naming of the images with the prefix EV (10.38).

EV 0.00 is the normal photograph with the custom settings we entered into the digital camera's Manual Settings.

EV -1.47 is the underexposed photograph and the EV+1.49 is the overexposed photograph.

☑ EV +1.49   ☑ EV 0.00   ☑ EV -1.47

(10.38)

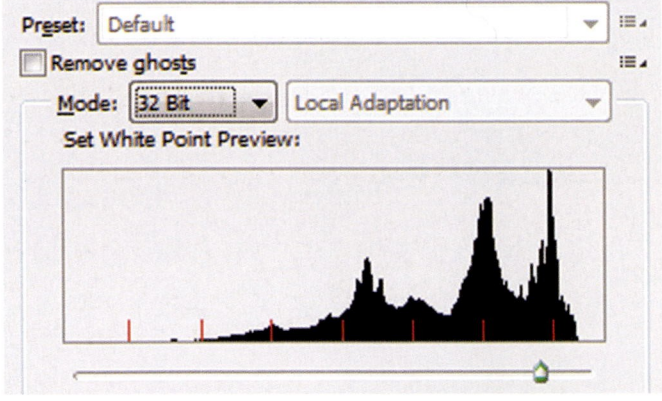

(10.39)

Over to the right you will see the Mode drop down menu, it is currently set to 16 Bit. We need to change this to 32 Bit. You will see that a histogram has loaded with a slider that can be adjusted (10.39).

This histogram is a function that will let you set the white point of the HDR file. You can drag the slider from left to right to see the effect it has on the preview image.

You can drag the slider to a position that best suits the image, we can make further changes after the file has been compiled using the HDR Toning option.

Press OK to finalize the process.

The final HDR image is now ready for you to edit and make refinements.

Go to the main menu and select Image, Adjustments, HDR Toning.

Try to make the same adjustments that you made to the bracketed panorama so that the images are as similar in tone as possible. I try to only adjust the sharpness, Color Vibrance, and the Saturation levels (10.40).

Finally save your file as a Radiance file .HDR. It may take 30 seconds or so to write the Radiance format.

Now we have both methods covered of shooting, processing and compiling custom photographs to act as lighting files, we can now progress to the final stage which is actually setting up a 3D Studio Max scene.

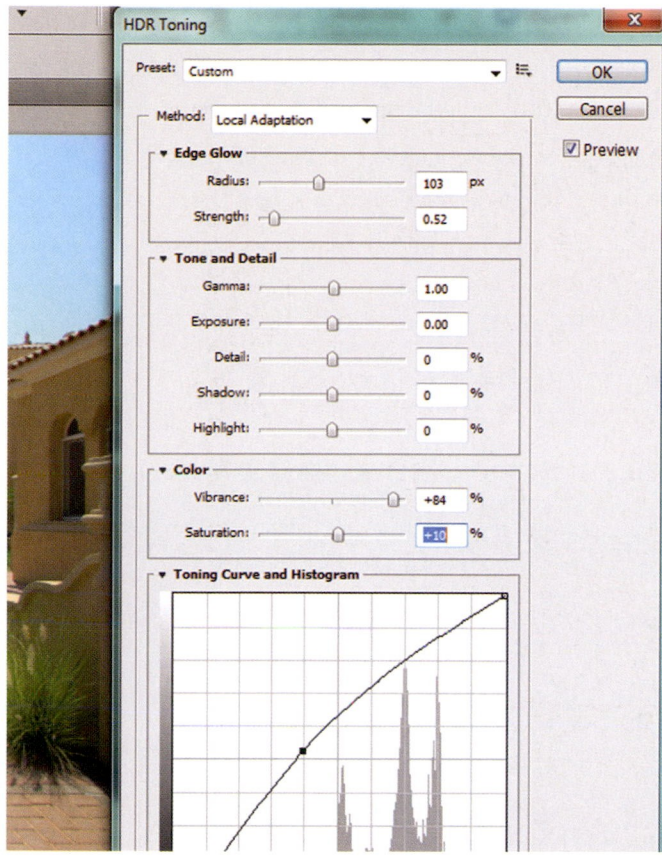

(10.40)

SETTING UP V-RAY HDRIS IN 3D STUDIO MAX

When I set up working project files in 3D Studio Max I become rather particular about what information is used and where it is stored.

There is no doubt that I like clean, workable files. I use one Max file for lighting and one file for all the modeling and texturing. This means that designers in my studio can access and work on the files individually and in a collaborative way.

Once my production model is ready I simply X-ref it into the lighting file or Light Rig as I call it and begin to render from there.

Let us progress now and set up the Light Rig.

Open up a fresh 3D Studio Max file.

Press F10 on your keyboard to bring up the Render Setup dialog box.

In here you we will need to make sure that the Output Size of the render matches the image size of our backplate. Simply enter the width and height values of your backplate which are 5184 × 3456 (10.41) .

Once you enter the values make sure that you lock off the Image Aspect ratio and the Pixel Aspect ratio. One you have

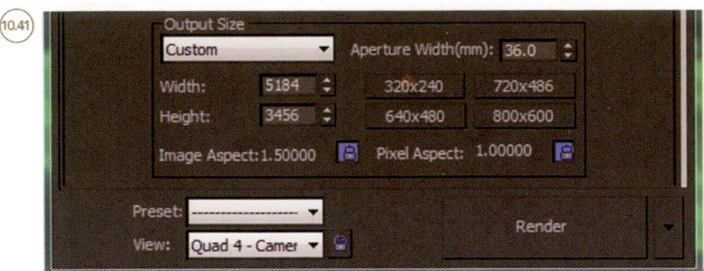

done this you can go ahead and enter a more reasonable output size for test renders. Set the width to 1000; you will see the Height will automatically adjust.

Scroll down to the Assign Renderer rollout. In here you need to set the Production renderer to V-Ray .

From the tabs at the top of the F10 dialog select the V-Ray tab 10.43.

From the rollouts select V-Ray:: Frame buffer. In here you need to enable the built-in Frame Buffer 10.44.

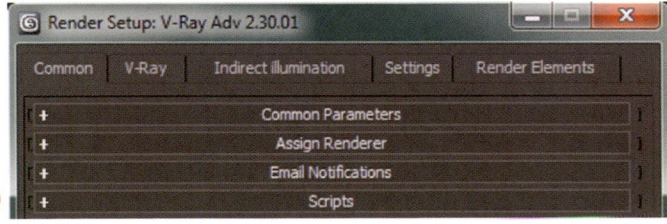

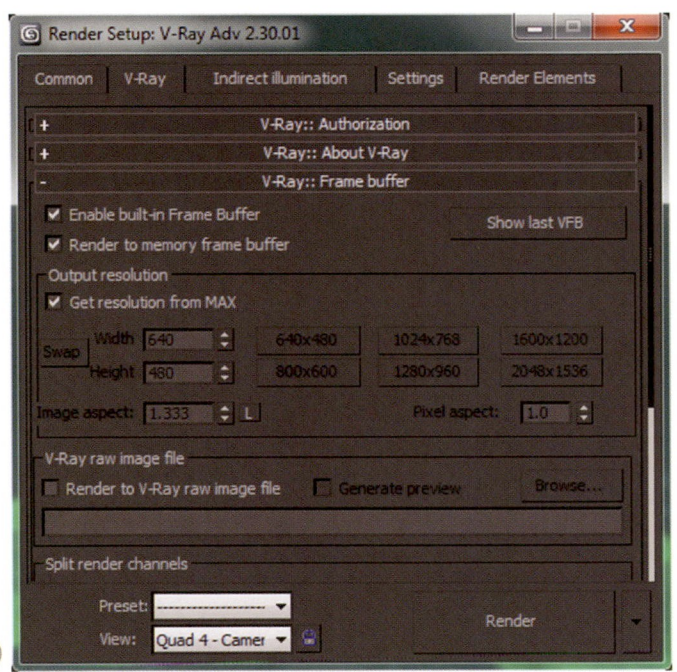

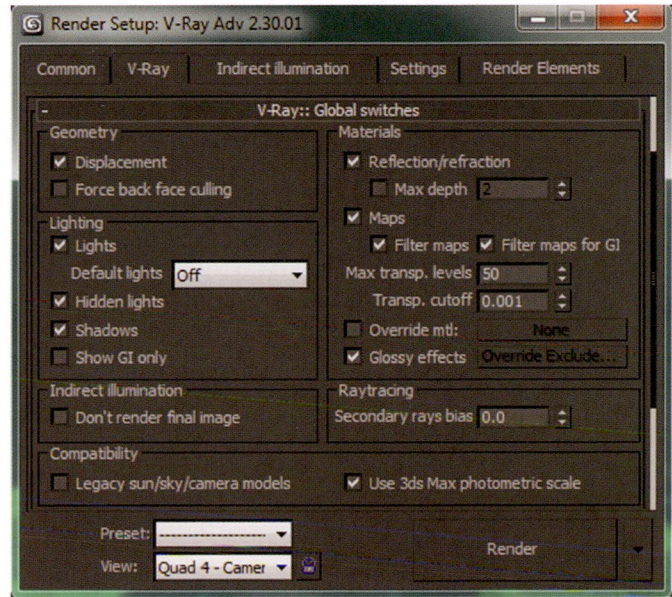

10.45

10.47

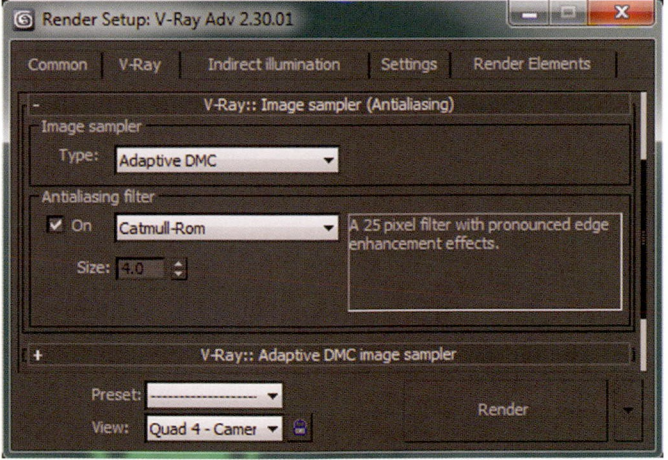

10.46

Next on the list is V-Ray:: Global switches. In the lighting section make sure the Default lights are set to Off. Also make sure Hidden lights is checked 10.45.

Just below the next rollout should be V-Ray:: Image Sampler. In here set the Image sampler Type to Adaptive DMC and the Antialiasing filter set to Catmull-Rom 10.46.

In the V-Ray:: Color mapping rollout, set the Type to Reinhard. Make sure the Sub-pixel mapping is checked as well as Clamp output and Affect background. Set the Burn value to 0.24 10.47.

In the next tab of the F10 dialog box is Indirect Illumination 10.48.

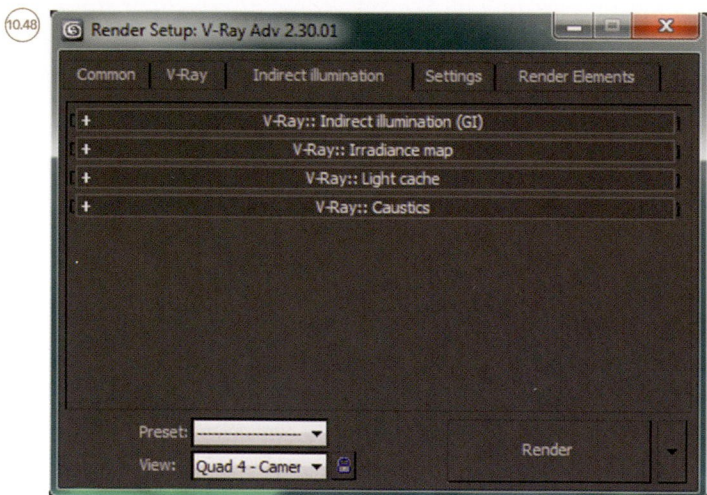

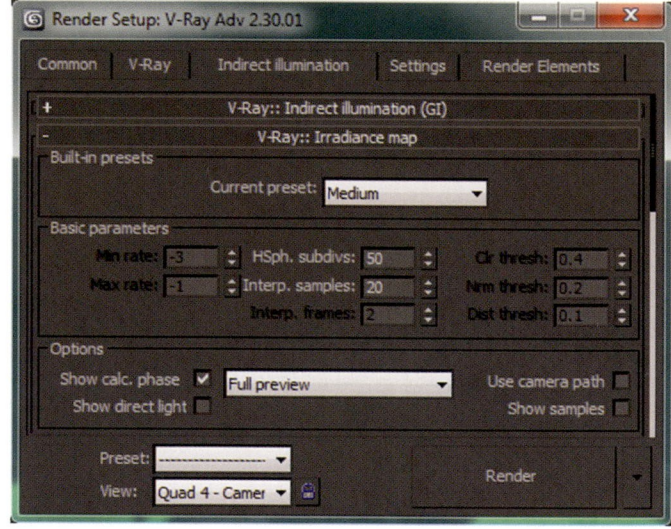

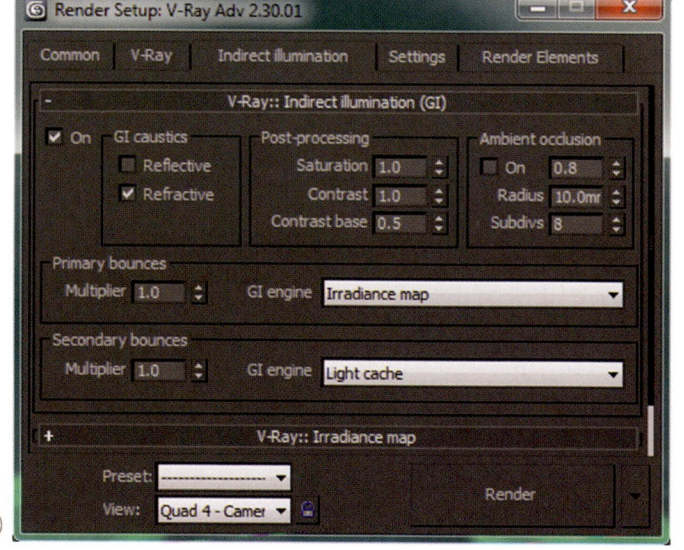

In the first rollout named V-Ray:: Indirect Illumination (GI) select the On.

Set the Primary bounces engine to Irradiance map.

Set the Secondary bounces engine to Light cache (10.49).

In the V-Ray:: Irradiance map rollout where Current preset is written, go ahead and select Medium from the drop down menu.

In the Options area make sure that Show calc. phase is enabled (10.50).

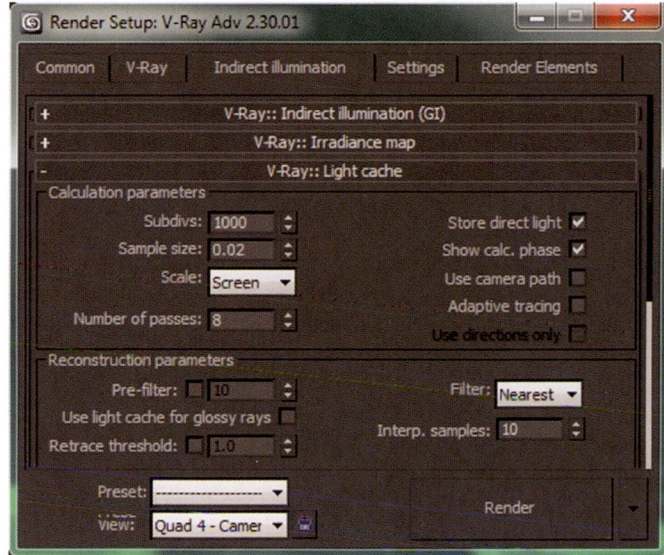

(10.51)

Set the Multiplier to a value of 2.4.

Scroll down to the light's options and make sure Invisible is checked as being active.

Just below you will find the Sampling options of the light. Enter a value of 30.0 in the Subdivs area.

In the Texture options area, enable the Use texture and set the Resolution to 2048.0.

Finally you need to scroll down to the Dome light options and select the Spherical (full dome).

We now need to import the panorama HDR file you created and apply it to the V-Ray Dome light.

Press M on your keyboard to bring up the Materials Editor. Import a new VRayHDRI file from the Material/Map Browser .

Finally scroll down to the V-Ray:: Light cache tab and adjust the Calculation parameters. In the Subdivs option set the value to 1000. The sample size is sufficient set to a value of 0.02. Make sure Show calc. phase is enabled (10.51)

Now the main settings have been applied we can set up the lighting elements. Bear in mind that HDR files are in a large format and bear a hefty weight which may affect your computer's response time.

Go ahead and create a V-Ray Dome Light. Place it anywhere in the scene.

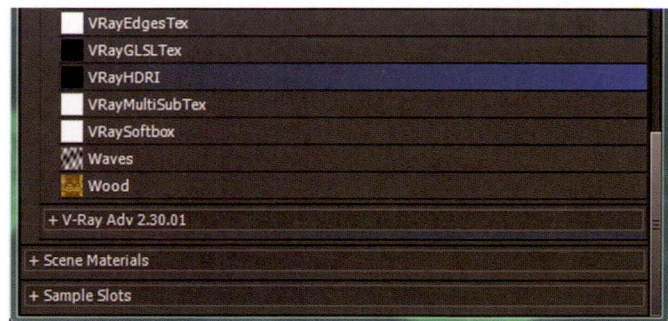

(10.52)

Once loaded, you will need to set the Mapping type to Spherical in the Mapping section of the shader's Parameters .

You will now need to drag and drop the HDRI preview image from the Material Editor dialog to the empty slot in the V-Ray Dome lights Texture options slot (10.54).

When the Instance Copy Method pop up appears be sure to select Instance and not Copy.

Now you have the Environment lighting ready and set, you will need to load a secondary HDRI file and instruct it to act as your backplate.

To do this we will be using another method of loading a HDR file. In a new Material slot import a Bitmap file from the Material/Map Browser (10.55).

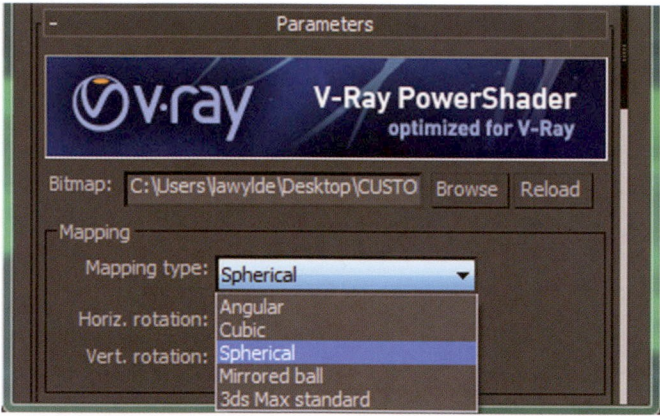

10.53

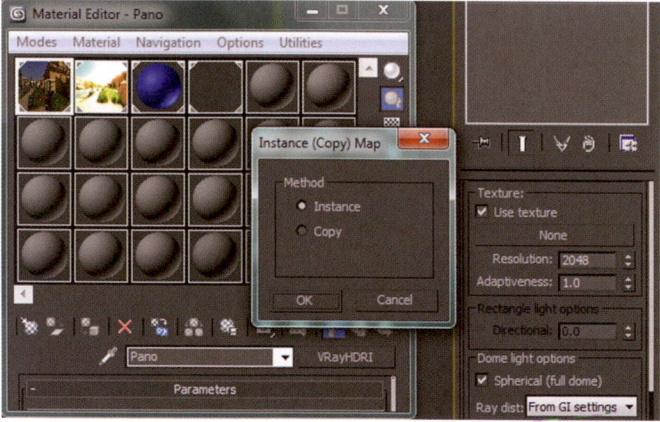

10.54

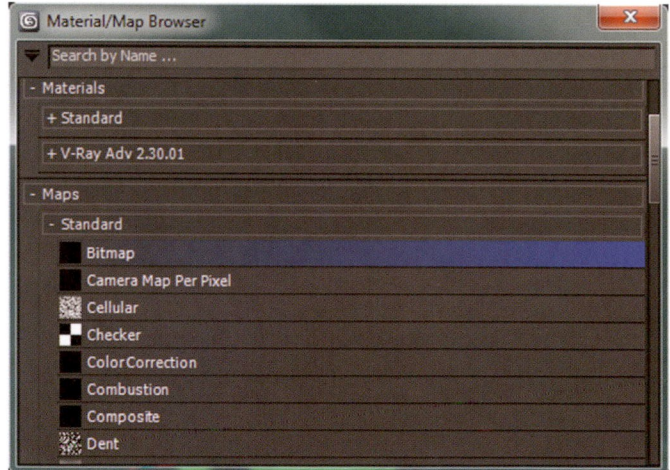

10.55

When it loads you will be prompted with an Explorer window, navigate to where the HDR files are stored and load in the BackPlate.hdr file that you created.

Once the HDR has loaded scroll down to the Coordinates rollout and switch the type from Texture to Environ. From the Mapping drop down menu choose Screen .

Now you have loaded the backplate you need to instruct V-Ray to use it as the visible background.

Press 8 on your keyboard to bring up the Environment and Effects dialog box.

In the Common Parameters section drag and drop the BackPlate.hdr into the empty Environment Map slot. Choose instance as the method of copying .

Now we have the main lighting rig set up we need to create a camera and some test geometry to make absolutely sure that the scene works properly and yields realistic results.

Let's go ahead and create a normal 3D Studio Max Camera.

Place the camera at the following coordinates 0,0,0. Make sure that the camera target is pointing straight ahead.

Select both the camera and its target and set the Z value to 1450 mm 10.58.

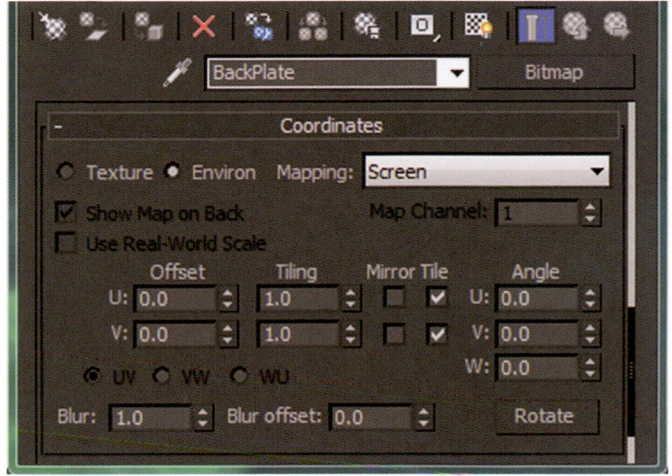

10.56

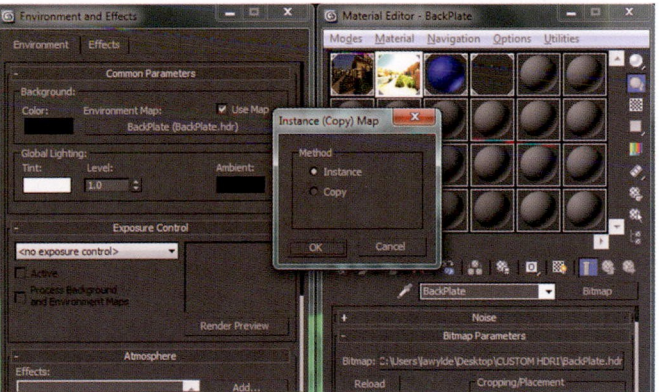

10.57

(10.58)

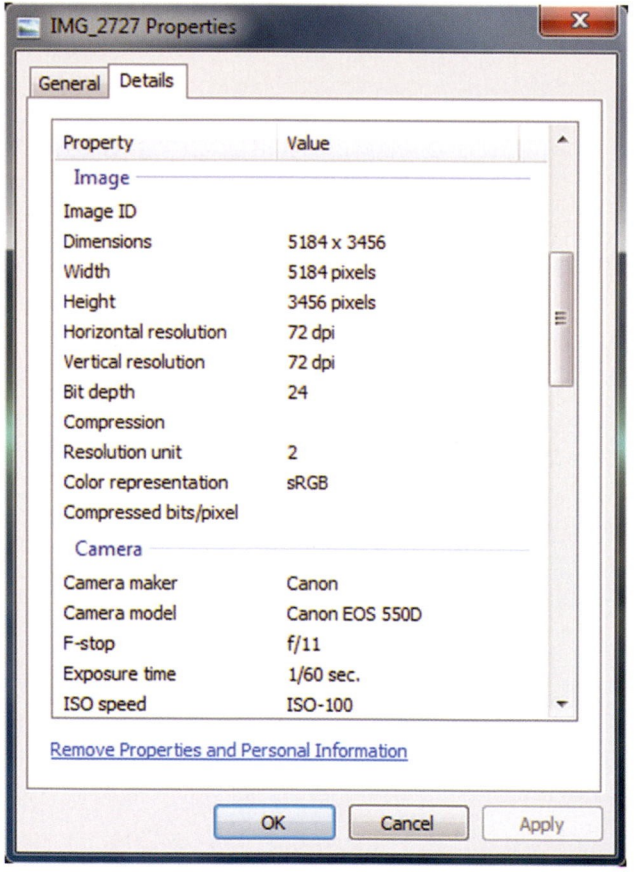

(10.59)

With only the camera selected navigate your way to its parameters. Match the lens to the one used on the digital SLR camera which is 10–20 mm. Sometimes geometry can look stretched and distorted due to the wrong focal depth being used. As everything is generally done by eye you can afford to make the odd adjustment in focal depth to suit your scene. If you are shooting backplates for your scenes then I would highly suggest using an alternative lens such as an 18–55 mm.

If in future you lose track of the type of lens you have used, you can check the photograph's properties in Windows Explorer (10.59).

Press C on your keyboard to go to the main camera view.

Press Shift + F on your keyboard, this will reveal the actual aperture that will be rendered.

Press F9 on your key board to produce a test render .

You will see that this is a pretty dark and dull output. Do not worry too much at this stage as we will be adjusting the levels to balance out the image.

At this stage it will be highly beneficial to see the backplate in your viewport so that you can place geometry ready for rendering.

To enable this feature, simply press Alt+B on your keyboard.

10.60

When the Viewport Configuration panel appears you need to select the Use Environment Background option. Press the Apply to Active View and then press OK 10.61.

Now that you can see the backplate, you can go ahead and create a piece of geometry. I use the built-in teapot as it can show accurate reflections on the curved surfaces. Insert as many teapots as you like.

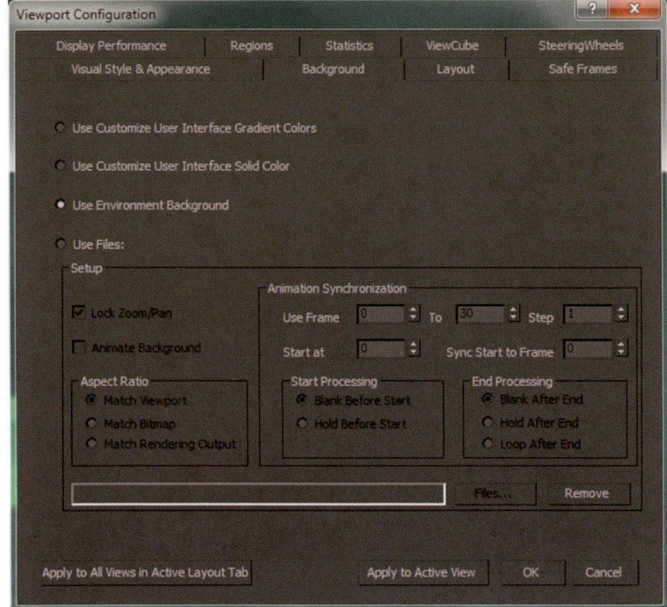

This is the geometry in my scene (10.62).

In order to produce a realistic render we need to apply realistic shaders to the geometry in the scene. We need to apply shaders that have reflective properties to make full use of the HDR lighting method.

Let's go ahead and apply a car paint material to the teapots. You can find this built in shader in the V-Ray material library. Once loaded in to the Materials palette you can apply the shader to the teapots (10.63).

We also need to make sure that the background HDR file looks a lot brighter than in the previous test render.

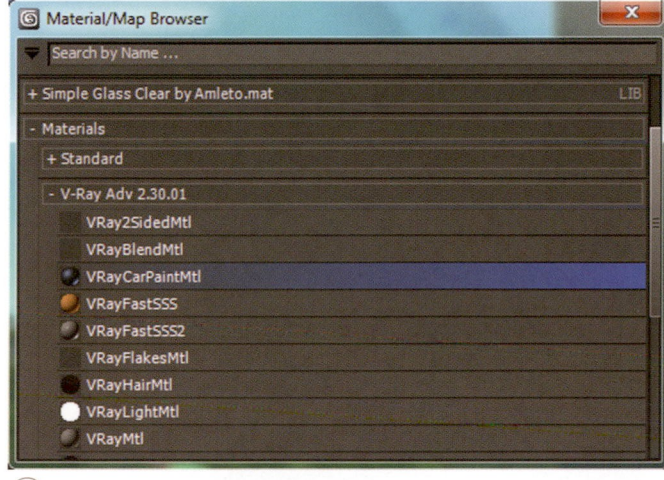

(10.63)

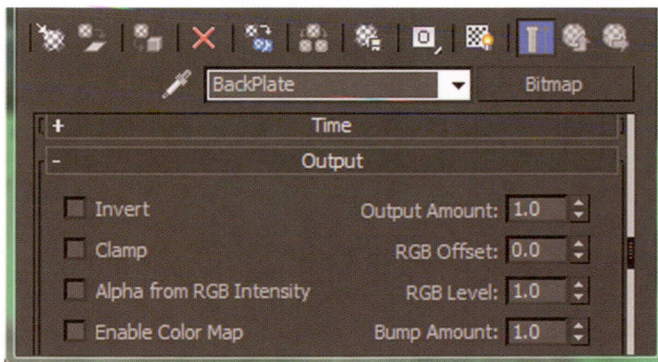

(10.64)

To do this open up the Materials Editor and scroll down to the Output rollout in the BackPlate Bitmap Material (10.64).

(10.65)

In here set the Output Amount to a value of 1.0. You should instantly see your viewport background change and become brighter.

We also need to make sure that the brightness of the reflections in the Panorama HDR file match the backplate so under Processing, adjust the Panorama's Overall mult. to a value of 4.0 (10.65).

Now would be a good time to see what results are being returned from the scene. Press F9 and produce a test render (10.66).

As you can see the render is showing significant signs of improvement.

You can see environmental shading and shadows; however in reality there would be direct shadows coming from the sun.

We also require a floor plane to receive the shadows yet its surface should remain invisible.

Let's start by creating a plane for the floor.

Create a plane from the Creation tool bar. Make sure the plane covers your foreground and enough area to pick up any geometry that you have created and to receive their associated direct shadow-casting paths 10.67.

In order for the floor to remain invisible during render time yet display proper shadow casting, we must apply a Matte/Shadow material to it.

Press M on your keyboard.

Import a new Matte/Shadow shader from the Standard library 10.68.

Apply the material to the plane object.

We also need to make sure that the ground plane is not visible in any reflections of the scene's geometry.

To do this we need to select the plane and right click on it. When the menu pops up choose Object Properties… 10.69.

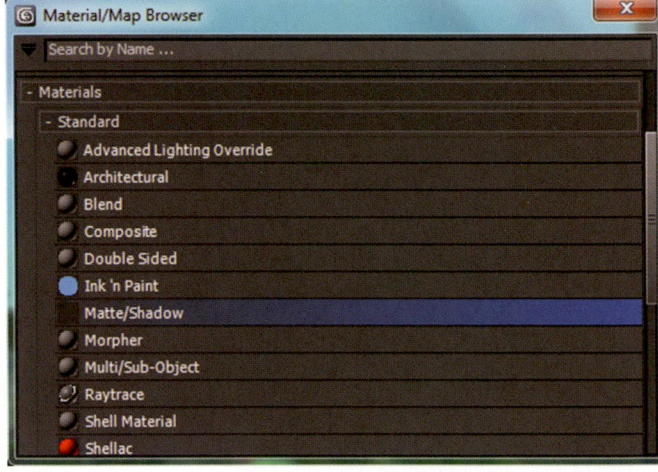

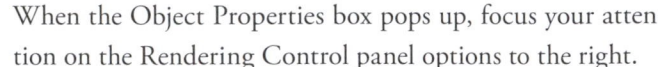

(10.68)

When the Object Properties box pops up, focus your attention on the Rendering Control panel options to the right.

You will need to uncheck the Visible to Reflection/Refraction option (10.70).

Now you can produce another test render to see if your ground plane works (10.71).

As you can see there are atmospheric shadowing details around the base of each tea pot. This is good and accurate enough for the scene type.

What we now need to do is create a V-Ray sun and position it correctly in order to match the position of the sun in the backplate.

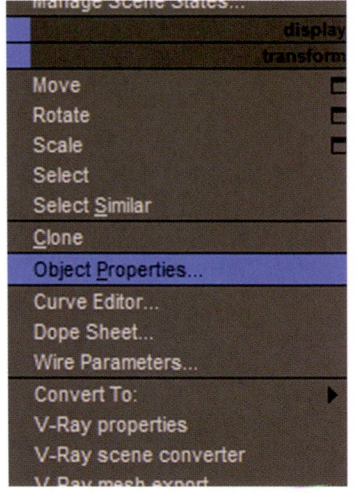

(10.69)

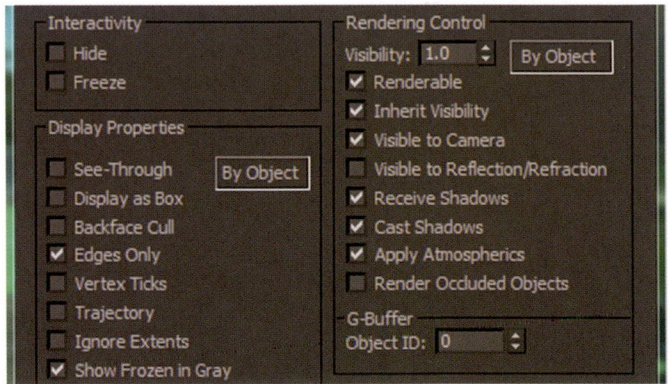

(10.70)

10.71

Create a V-Ray sun and position it as best you can to match the backplate. Pay attention to the way the shadows fall from the architecture of the scene. You can refine the placement of the sun in your camera view (10.72).

You now need to change a few settings to the V-Ray Sun in the Modification panel.

First change the Intensity multiplier to a value of 0.15.

Change the Photon emit radius to 20,000.

Once you are happy with the final position of the V-Ray Sun go ahead and produce a test render (10.73).

For a final production shot you may want to increase the final render size together with the Irradiance map and Light cache settings to suit.

As you can see the results can be incredibly realistic and creatively very rewarding.

This type of workflow is ideal for vehicle rendering and product rendering etc.

Here is an example of what can be achieved with this method of capturing bracketed photographs, manipulating them and putting them to functional use in 3D Studio Max and V-Ray (10.74).

(10.74)

FINAL THOUGHTS

Using Autodesk 3D Max with V-Ray as the rendering engine can provide you with a very powerful set of tools to aid you in your career. I hope this book has refined and improved your understanding of how these software packages intertwine to provide realistic results. It is now your turn to create visuals and improve your portfolio. I do intend writing a book containing advanced 3D Studio Max and V-Ray tools such as automation in rendering and advanced lighting effects. For now, keep practicing and I look forward to any technical inquiries or tutorial requests,

Lee Wylde

INDEX

DATE DUE
